What Others A

'Arianna has been a personal friend for over 28 years and we have watched how she has given her life in every season to helping others find the pearl hidden beneath the pain. This book is both practical and hope-filled, so let its pages push you into your promises.'
Steve and Charlotte Gambill, Life Church, Bradford, England

'Arianna Walker and her work with Mercy Ministries UK is a huge inspiration. From Pain to Pearls is full of hope – a book of transformation and revelation that will leave you feeling empowered to embrace a process of change from the inside out.'
Nicky and Pippa Gumbel, Holy Trinity Brompton, London, England

'We have watched Arianna grow in Godly wisdom and stature as she gives selflessly to the hurting and vulnerable in compassion and service; this book encapsulates so much of what she has learnt as she brings healing to broken hearts and lives. As Jesus taught in parables, so she has found ways to express and illustrate deep truths that everyone can benefit from. We thoroughly recommend this book, it will be a light for those who are in darkness and a manual for those who pray for and counsel them.'
John and Anne Coles, New Wine, UK

'From Pain to Pearls' is a beacon of hope – an easy to read, practical manual for healing, peace, help, strength and so much more. Arianna is a gift to us all and we thoroughly recommend her book.'
Matt and Beth Redman

'Arianna's loving heart for people and her passion for everyone to find freedom in Christ, brings forth great insights throughout the whole book. Whatever circumstances and experiences may have shaped you, Arianna's

I

practical way of describing how to rise up and move forward is down-to-earth and easy to grasp, making it relevant to everyone. Thank you Arianna for your courage and willingness to write a book so filled with love, wisdom and faith.'
Jarle and Merete Tangstad, Church in The Culture Center, Copenhagen, Denmark

From Pain To Pearls

Arianna Walker

Presence Books

Copyright © Arianna Walker, 2014
First published in Great Britain by Presence Books in 2014

ISBN: 978-1-907228-33-9

Presence Books, Eastbourne

Dedication

This book is dedicated to my sister Debbie whose determined faith, ruthless trust and uncompromising hope in God is a constant source of inspiration to me. Her story of turning pain into pearls has intertwined with my own and together we have seen the mighty hand of God bring healing, restoration and transformation to many lives.

Genesis 50:20

'You intended to harm me, but God intended it for good to accomplish what is now being done, the saving of many lives.'

VI

Acknowledgements

No project like this is ever achieved alone: there are many people who I will be eternally indebted to for their input, encouragement, support and friendship and without whom this book would never have made it out of my heart and onto these pages.

Thank you to Natalie Rees and Christine Gilland for your edits, grammar checks and turning my paragraph-long sentences into something more readable. Thanks also to Pastor Stephen Matthew for ensuring what I wrote was actually scriptural! Thanks to Dave Roberts and all at Presence for your logistical support and willingness to pull this off at speed. Thanks also to Bruce Mytton for a beautiful cover.

Thanks to Mark, Gemma, Karen and Rob for being prepared to share your pearls of great price. Overcoming adversity and responding with *nacre* to coat the pain and bring forth healing is never easy, but you have shown that it is worth it. Thank you for your honesty and courage and for the hope that your stories bring.

To my husband Matthew: thank you for believing I can do anything and reminding me of that when I doubt myself. Thank you also for being true to your promise of living an adventure together – I'm loving every minute!

To my boys Jacob and Sol: you two mean more to me than words can say. Thank you for being so generous with me as your Mum – your willingness to come on this journey and embrace every aspect of our crazy family life has enabled us all to keep growing. I'm so very proud of you and love spending time with you both. Together will always be the best place to be.

To my friends: you know who you are. Life is indeed better with friends and I am forever grateful for the wisdom, the laughter, the silly games, the tears, the prayers and the late night chats of hopes and dreams shared together.

To Nancy Alcorn: thank you for your constant support, belief and empowerment. You are one of my heroes, a great inspirational leader and a very dear friend.

To Steve and Charlotte Gambill, my pastors and my friends. Thank you for loving me just as I am, whilst encouraging me to keep stepping out and to keep saying yes. Thank you for leading by example and teaching me how to work hard, play hard and rest hard. Oh, and for the yurting…

And finally to my Heavenly Father: words are not enough and so instead I will live from a grateful heart all the days of my life to bring glory to Your Name.

Contents

x

Introduction

Life is not perfect.

My sister was 12 years old when she met a man in the local park. He was 10 years her senior, drove his own car, and showed an interest in her that made her feel grown-up and affirmed. Within the space of a few short weeks, he had groomed her into a sexual relationship with him. Only then did it become apparent that he was a drug dealer, and that he had plans for my sister that took her from the dream life she had been living into a living hell.

Every day for three years, life was the same — hidden with the same lie that 'all was fine'. But it wasn't. She got into fights, began cutting herself, became addicted to drugs, and even tried to commit suicide. Caught in a spiral of helplessness and shame, her anger burned against a God who should have protected her, who could have stopped it, or who could have told someone about the abuse she was suffering. She felt let down by Him, abandoned even, and so she renounced God and vowed to live her life without Him.

My sister and I, along with our three siblings, were brought up in a loving, Christian home, with parents who were missionaries and pastors for many years. Looking back, I think we grew up with an underlying belief system that 'bad things happen to bad people'. We took refuge in the idea that we were good people and not *of* this world (John 17:16), and were therefore exempt from its pain. But we failed to understand that if we are *in* this world, then we can be victims of its corruption. So when, as a family, we saw the full scale of what my sister had been through, it shook our world and our faith.

My sister is doing great now. After years of turmoil and pain, she finally got to a point where she asked for help. She ended up becoming the first girl from the UK to be accepted into Mercy Ministries of America when she was 18 years old, and it started a journey of discovering truth. She allowed God the space and time to speak for Himself. He shared His thoughts with her about what had happened to her and taught her how to reconcile the facts of her past with the truth of the future He had planned.

Mercy Ministries was founded by Nancy Alcorn in the U.S.A., in 1983. After many years of working in women's prisons and with the social services, she realised that without a Christ-centred approach, the cycle of destruction in the lives of those around her would continue.

Now, over three decades later, Mercy Ministries runs homes across the world, offering a six-month residential programme that, with God at the centre, transforms the lives of young women between the ages of 18 and 28 who are facing life-controlling issues such as depression, eating disorders, self-harm and the emotional effects of abuse. The Mercy Ministries' programme is voluntary, Christ-centered and completely free of charge. It has been my honour and privilege to be part of pioneering this great ministry in the UK.

Mercy Ministries UK opened its doors to young women on September 4th, 2006 and since then, we have seen God reveal to girl after girl the power that comes from learning to apply the truth of God's word to every wound; to see God's unconditional love, forgiveness and life-transforming power turn their pain into pearls of great value.

My sister Debbie is married now, with two children. She is serving God with all her heart and what's more, she is the Programme Director at Mercy Ministries UK. I have the privilege of working alongside her every day, seeing countless young women's lives rescued from hopelessness and despair into the loving arms of a God whose love conquers all.

My sister's story has impacted my life like no other; I had to go on a journey of discovering what the Bible says about God's character and find my own answer to that age-old question: 'Where is God when it hurts?' How do we respond when bad things happen to good people, and how can we learn to 'Laugh at the days to come' (Proverbs 31:25) when our future is so unknown? Can we trust Him with the things we love the most? And if God does not promise us a trouble-free life, then what exactly does He promise?

This book, *From Pain To Pearls,* is my response to these questions. I'm not saying it's *the* response, only that it is mine. During the years at Mercy Ministries UK, and over the past 20 years serving within my local church context, I have stood alongside countless people as they have navigated some of the worst kinds of things life can throw at a person — rape, abuse, torture, incest, betrayal, grief, shame, debt, loneliness and ill health.

I have felt the raging seas of my own personal trials, tribulations and adversities of life, and yet discovered the stepping-stones of faith, hope, trust and unconditional love, that have paved a safe way through the trials. I have learnt to, 'Never be afraid to trust an unknown future to a known God' as Corrie ten Boom famously said. And I want to share that journey with you.

As you read this book, my prayer is that you will discover the tools that God has made available, through Jesus Christ, to equip and empower us to rise from a victim position and become more than survivors of troubled lives; to step into our new lives as overcomers, living in the fullness of the freedom that Christ died for us to have. My prayer is that you learn what it means to turn every trial, challenge, and troubled situation from a pain into a pearl.

Arianna Walker

January 2014

Chapter 1: Equipped For Rough Terrain

Snow is good for skiing. Or sledging. Or building snow men. Or snowball fights and snow angels. That's what snow is good for. It's *not* good for driving in. It's 8am in the middle of winter and my street looks like a winter wonderland – except for the scene of complete carnage and chaos, that is.

One of my neighbours is digging her car out in her high heels; another one has managed to get half-way up our hill but now his car is stuck and is rolling threateningly backwards; whilst a third has decided to try the 'just put your foot down' approach, ignoring the pleading screech and whine of his tyres as he moves approximately 4cm before giving up and going back inside.

I watch the scene for a moment before I put on my coat and snow boots, clear my windscreen, get in my car, turn on the engine and press a special button with a big 'W' on it. I can see my neighbours look up and stop as they watch my car glide out of my drive and up our steep hill without so much as a slip or a slide; each tyre gripping the snow like it was brand new tarmac.

You see, my car was built for rough terrain. It has features that ensure challenging terrain is navigated smoothly and with every possible chance of success. Everyone on my street was faced with the same scenario. The same conditions had been inflicted on us all by the snowfall, and yet those conditions did not stop me from getting where I needed to be because I was properly equipped, powered up and well-protected by what was carrying me.

Did you know that you were built, designed and equipped to navigate the rough terrain of your life and of the world in the same way?

Yet so often, we try to make it through our lives with the same approach my neighbours had to the challenges of rough terrain. Some of us are busy digging our lives out of the snow and exhausting our resources because we are doing it in our own strength; some of us make a little progress and then glide right back to where we started; still others just put their foot down, go for it with everything they've got, only to realise they're not going anywhere, and so they give up and go inside.

We cannot have a belief system built on the misconception that our status of 'Christian' is an automatic exemption from adversity and trials.

There may be trouble ahead

The thing is, snow happens. In my part of the world it happens nearly every winter, and yet every winter, our entire city comes to a standstill at the slightest snow flurry; as if somehow we are surprised it's come to taunt us again. We don't like the way the roads become slippery; we don't like the cold, or the fact that we have to park on main roads and leave extra time to get to work. We don't like the long queues caused by the rough terrain, and we definitely don't like those individuals who continue to drive like maniacs, who will be a likely cause of the next accident.

Life is very much like this analogy. The world we live in has rough terrain called hurt, pain, fear, abuse, betrayal, disappointment, rebellion, mistrust and injustice, to name but a few. And whilst we don't have to like it, we do need to respond to it.

When Jesus commissioned us to: 'Go out into all the world and preach the good news' (Mark 16:15), He knew the world would not give us a nice, smooth, tarmac road, but that life in this world would present us with mud, rocks, hills and valleys.

In 1 Thessalonians 3:3-5 Paul writes:

> 'Not that the troubles should come as any surprise to you. You've always known that we're in for this kind of thing. It's part of our calling. When we were with you, we made it quite clear that there was trouble ahead.' (The Message)

The 'trouble ahead' is not because God is punishing us. The trouble ahead is part of our living environment, our earth, which is still struggling under the weight of sin and corruption. Trouble can come from us being the victims of other people's bad choices; it can come from our own ignorance and disobedience; and it can come through no fault of our own, sent by an enemy who comes to 'kill, steal and destroy' us (John 10:10).

We cannot have a belief system built on the misconception that our status of 'Christian' is an automatic exemption from adversity and trials.

In fact, the reality is that James 1 indicates that we will 'Face trials of many kinds'; no exemptions are implied! What those

3

trials develop in us though, depends entirely on how we respond to them and on how we view God's part in it all.

God is not the source of our pain

If we believe that somehow God is responsible for our pain, if we believe that He is the source of it, either as a punishment for our failings, or by His perceived unwillingness to intervene, then He cannot become the resource for our healing. If this is what we believe in our minds, we will feel unsafe around Him. How can we turn to someone for help and strength when a part of us is wondering if He is somehow the cause, the source, or the reason why we are suffering?

I know I have been guilty of fearfully suspecting that God would send pain in order to teach me a lesson, to teach me how to overcome, how to grow. I thought that in order for me to know Him as my rescuer, He could be capable of sending disaster. One time, when I was questioning His motives towards me, when I feared the lengths He might go to, to 'grow' me, I heard Him say to me: 'Would you throw your children into the fire to teach them that it is hot?'

Seeing this from the point of view of a loving parent, with all the feeling of love and protection I feel towards my children, helped me to see God's perspective. The fact is, I would NEVER throw my children into the fire to teach them that it's hot, and neither would our heavenly Father do the same to you or me. But fire does exist, and as a loving parent, I need to teach my children that fire can burn. So what do I do? I tell them that it is hot. I show them how to respond to fire.

I teach them the dangers of matches and how to minimise the chances of getting burnt. I may move them close to the fire so that they can feel its heat; not close enough to burn but close enough to understand what heat feels like. I know that my children would then have a choice to make, just like we do.

Some may listen to the warnings and apply the instructions, and so learn how to avoid or extinguish the flames. But some may fall into the fire by mistake; some may choose not to listen and decide that they want to learn the hard way, through the consequences of their own power to choose. Some are maliciously pushed into the fire by others; and sometimes the fire may simply explode or increase to the point that we are burned by it, despite our best attempts to avoid it. Such is the nature of fire; such is the nature of trouble in our lives. But it's the nature of our Father that we should be clear on: He is good. Full stop. He is love. Full stop. He is kind. Full stop.

He cannot give what He does not possess. Yes, He has wrath and judgement and anger and frustration: just read the Old Testament and you will see it filled with examples of God's need to punish disobedience, sin and rebellion. But fast-forward to the New Testament, and you will find that Jesus became the means by which God satisfies His need for judgement and wrath. He pinned it all on His own Son for our sake, for our benefit, so that we could come to know Him as the source of our healing, the source of our strength; the source of our peace, our patience, our wisdom, and our ability to endure and persevere under the trials that He knows will come.

'Every good and perfect gift comes from the Lord' (James 1:17). If it's not good, it's not from God! When we can accurately identify the fact that our heavenly Father is not the source of pain, then He can become the resource for our healing. Yes, bad things can happen to good people, but blaming God for evil is like blaming the sun for darkness.

In the introduction to this book, I recount my sister Debbie's story. Her story is not unique; I know many of us have faced times in our lives where the character of God and His intentions towards us are called into question by the circumstances we face. It's a very common way for the enemy to separate us from God.

He gets us to call God's character, motivation and intention towards us into question. Satan does what he can to undermine who God is: to put a hint of doubt in our hearts as to His goodness, His mercy, His kindness and His love. Because if the enemy can succeed in sowing doubt in our minds, if he can cause us to see God as unsafe, then he can disrupt our flow with God causing mistrust, doubt and fear to enter in. He has done this successfully from the very beginning of time.

We may not always be able to control what happens to us, but we can control how we respond.

Genesis 3:1-5 shows us how subtle the enemy's poison can be:

> 'Now the serpent was more crafty than any of the wild animals the Lord God had made. He said to the woman, "Did God really say, 'You must not eat from any tree in the garden'?"
>
> The woman said to the serpent, "We may eat fruit from the trees in the garden, but God did say: 'You must not eat fruit from the tree that is in the middle of the garden, and you must not touch it, or you will die.'"

"You will not certainly die," the serpent said to the
woman. "For God knows that when you eat from it
your eyes will be opened, and you will be like God,
knowing good and evil.'"

In this conversation, we see the serpent present God as a liar;
as a God that is somehow insecure and worried that humanity
could become like Him. The serpent presents God's motive
for forbidding Adam and Eve access to the tree as nothing to
do with their protection, but instead, as a way to keep them
small.

Adam and Eve's failure to trust the God they knew, and instead
believe a subtle lie about His nature, His character, His
motivation and intention towards them, caused untold
devastation for all of humankind, and played right into Satan's
hands. We may not always be able to control what happens to
us, but we can control how we respond.

The fact is, that all along God has had a plan in place to help
us, His people, with a right response to wrong things, through a
relationship with Jesus Christ. He has made us able to respond
to hurt, pain, challenge, abuse, trauma and adversity in a way
that releases us from the destructive effects of these things.

We are the body of Christ, and He needs His body healthy and
whole so that we can move and run and reach out to build His
Kingdom. He has equipped us with His Holy Spirit, and
through our relationship with Him we can turn every tear, hurt,
trauma, heartache and pain into a pearl.

From violation to value

Have you ever eaten an oyster? Personally, I can't think of

anything worse than prying open a shell and then slurping up a blob of a salty, slimy sea creature — but I'm told they are a delicacy. Having said that, whatever I might think of oysters as a menu option, I have to say I'm pretty impressed with them as jewellers!

Oysters are the living organisms responsible for producing pearls. Unlike gemstones or precious metals that have to be mined from the earth, pearls are grown inside live oysters far below the surface of the sea.

Gemstones (like diamonds and rubies) have to undergo a long process of cutting and polishing to bring out their beauty; but pearls need no such treatment to reveal their loveliness. It's the only gem in the world that is produced by a living organism.

Unless the oyster remembers its God given ability to respond to pain, to adversity and trial, it will slowly die.

Oysters live in harsh terrain: in the ocean or in rivers where all sorts of dangers lurk. Grains of sand, parasites or sharp pieces of shell can find their way past the oyster's hard outer shell and into the fleshy, soft tissue of the living organism. When this happens, the oyster has a novel way of responding to the intrusion: it produces something called *nacre* (nā'kər).

Nacre is sometimes known as 'mother of pearl' in reference to the fact that the very substance of a pearl is made up of layer upon layer of nacre. So oysters can turn an obstruction, an irritant, a violation, into a precious jewel, by secreting this substance and covering the irritant, rounding its sharp edges until it can no longer cause damage.

I just love God's creativity; not only did He create oysters with the ability to protect themselves, they were going to do it in style! The sad fact is that only about 50% of oysters that have an irritant or obstruction lodge inside of them produce a pearl. When an oyster fails to produce nacre, it risks everything.

The obstruction, whether it's a grain of sand or a small piece of broken shell, will often have sharp edges; and so it will begin to cut away and erode the soft tissue — the living part of the oyster. Or if it's a parasite that enters, it will gradually gnaw away at the inside of the oyster until there is nothing left.

Unless the oyster remembers its God given ability to respond to pain, to adversity and trial, it will slowly die. It will slowly erode and eventually become nothing but an empty shell. I know people who feel just like that: empty shells.

The fact is, like the oyster, God has created us with the spiritual equivalent of nacre. We have a natural ability to respond to pain, to hurt, to offense, to trauma and to abuse that will cause these violations to halt their destructive path on the inside of us; instead, producing something of great value.

Formed in the secret place

The thing about pearls that I find really interesting is that they are formed hidden away in a secret place. No one sees the nacre being secreted by the oyster. No one sees the pearl until it's fully formed. *It's an entirely internal process, and so it is for us.*

From Pain to Pearls

What goes on, on the inside of our being — in our hearts, in our minds, wills and emotions, will set the tone for our behaviours.

We will produce on the outside what we release on the inside.

We will produce on the outside what we release on the inside. Each chapter of this book will look at different nacre responses that we can release on the inside of us, that will help to protect the very life of our being.

We can choose to be an oyster that learns to release the spiritual equivalent of nacre and so turn our pain into a pearl, or we can choose not to do that, and like the oyster, be slowly chewed up by whatever has violated our heart. In the end, it will be like death to us.

Before I go into more detail about each type of nacre response that we can produce, I want to point out that a pearl is formed in layers. It's not a one-time release; the oyster does not secrete the nacre for a set amount of time: it releases the nacre continuously until the sharp edge of whatever threatened its life has been completely and totally and thoroughly rounded and softened, so as to cause no more damage.

It's the same with us. We can't just forgive once, or go to church once, or worship once, or pray once; we have to be willing to embark on a process; a commitment to keep releasing whatever we need to, whatever our nacre happens to be at the time, for it to produce that pearl.

10

And for us to be able to do that, we need to start from a place of trust in God. We have to be able to trust that He is taking us and leading us along. We have to believe in His ability to turn our pain into something of value.

From Pain to Pearls

Chapter 2: The God Of 'Instead'

God is in the business of divine exchange; just read Isaiah 61:3:

> '...to bestow on them a crown of beauty instead of ashes, the oil of joy instead of mourning, and a garment of praise instead of a spirit of despair.'

The very first step of releasing nacre, of being strengthened enough inside of ourselves to be able to respond to whatever has violated us, is to come to a place of trust in our Father God. This is why it's so important to know *who* He is; to know His character. Because if you think He is in any way the source of your pain, He cannot become the resource for your healing.

As the oyster releases nacre, so too must our hearts release trust, and with it, everything that is holding us back from trusting Him completely.

There's a famous story about a little girl and her pearl necklace. Maybe you've heard it before, but in case you haven't, let me share it:

> The cheerful girl with bouncy brunette curls was almost five. Waiting with her mother at the checkout stand, she saw them — a circle of glistening white pearls in a pink, foil box – 'Oh please, Mummy...can I have them? Please, Mummy, please!'

> Quickly the mother checked the back of the little foil box and then looked back into the pleading brown eyes of her little girl's upturned face. '£1.95 – that's almost £2.00. If you really want them, I'll think of some extra

chores for you, and in no time, you can save enough money to buy them for yourself. And don't forget it's your birthday soon, you may even get a little extra then.'

As soon as the young girl got home, she emptied her piggy bank and counted out 17 pennies. After dinner, she did more than her share of chores and she even went to the neighbour and asked if she could pick weeds for 10p.

On her birthday, her Grandma kindly gave her £1, and at last she had enough money to buy the necklace. Oh how she loved her pearls. They made her feel dressed up and grown up. She wore them everywhere: school, garden, playground, even to bed. The only time she took them off was when she went swimming or had a bubble bath. Her Mum had told her that if they got wet, they might turn her neck green.

This little girl was blessed with a very loving Daddy, and every night when she was ready for bed, he would stop whatever he was doing and come upstairs to read her a story. One night when he finished the story, he asked her: 'Do you love me?'
'Oh yes, Daddy. You know that I love you.'
'Then give me your pearls.'
'Oh, Daddy, not my pearls. But you can have Princess, the white horse from my collection – the one with the pink tail. Remember, Daddy? The one you gave me. She's my favourite.'

'That's okay, honey. Daddy loves you. Good night.' And he brushed her cheek with a kiss.

About a week later, after the story time, her Daddy asked again, 'Do you love me?'

'Daddy, you know I love you.'

'Then give me your pearls.'

'Oh Daddy, not my pearls. But you can have my baby doll – the brand new one I got for my birthday. She is so beautiful, and you can have the yellow blanket that matches her sleeper.'

'That's okay. Sleep well. God bless you, little one. Daddy loves you.' And as always, he brushed her cheek with a gentle kiss.

A few nights later when her Daddy came in, the little girl was sitting on her bed with her legs crossed. As he came close, he noticed her chin was trembling and one silent tear rolled down her cheek.

'What is it, sweetheart? What's the matter?'

Without a word, she lifted her little hand up to her Daddy. And when she opened it, there was her little pearl necklace. With a little quiver, she finally said, 'Here, Daddy. It's for you.'

With tears gathering in his own eyes, her kind Daddy reached out with one hand to take the bargain-store necklace, and with the other hand, he reached into his pocket and pulled out a blue velvet case, with a strand of genuine pearls. These were precious pearls, expensive and genuine, softly glowing in the dim light of her room; and as she took hold of them, she knew without a doubt that he had given her treasure instead of trash…

This story is a modern day parable — it reveals the Father's heart towards us, and the power there is in trusting Him

15

enough to lay down the things we feel we need to, want to, have to, keep hold of.

The artificial stabilisers of life can be anything we are holding onto that God has asked us to trust Him with.

Removing the stabilisers

The trouble is, that many of us struggle to let go. We could compare those things that we hold onto with the artificial stabilisers we put on a child's bike to help them stay upright and balanced. Our lives can be like that bike — artificially held up by stabilisers that we have put there to help us feel safe, to feel balanced, to feel like we can make it through another day.

Those artificial stabilisers of life can be anything we are holding onto that God has asked us to trust Him with. Maybe it's people, a best friend, a relative, a husband or a wife. Maybe it's our job, our title or position, our roles and responsibilities, or our financial status that gives us a sense of stability and security.

For some, their artificial stabilisers are more destructive — eating disorders, self-harm, addictions; all of these behaviours are artificial ways of keeping a life upright, of helping us feel as if we are in control, when in fact all we are doing is restricting God's ability to teach us how to ride!

Humanity has found its own ways to fill the God-shaped hole inside of us.

We have found our own ways to cope with the pressures and uncertainties of life; and we have found our own ways to stay in control, to stay upright on the bike of our lives.

God is asking for us to trust Him by letting go of the things we have put in place ourselves.

But they are artificial ways, and they will eventually restrict, constrict, and keep your life small; and even though you may feel like you are peddling your bike with great momentum, you'll find with artificial stabilisers on, your progress will be hampered.

Everybody needs to feel a sense of belonging, acceptance, significance and control, but if you find those things outside of your relationship with God, if they are artificial ways of keeping your balance and stability in life, then there will come a point when you realise that those stabilisers are just too restrictive. They hold you back, restrict your speed, and prevent you from being able to explore all the terrain life has to offer; because artificial stabilisers are designed for small bikes – small lives – and that is not what God has called His people to have.

God is asking for us to trust Him by letting go of the things we have put in place ourselves: every self-generated coping mechanism, every defense mechanism, every artificial stabiliser, and *instead* to trust Him to teach us His way of responding to life's challenges. If we let Him, He will teach us the wonder of learning to ride the bike of our lives without the restriction of stabilisers. He will teach us to ride in total freedom.

Let me take you to the story of the rich young ruler, which, in light of my artificial stabiliser analogy, just seems a perfect illustration. It's found in the book of Matthew:

> 'Another day, a man stopped Jesus and asked, "Teacher, what good thing must I do to get eternal life?" Jesus said, "Why do you question me about what's good? God is the One who is good. If you want to enter the life of God, just do what he tells you." The man asked, "What in particular?" Jesus said, "Don't murder, don't commit adultery, don't steal, don't lie, honour your father and mother, and love your neighbour as you do yourself." The young man said, "I've done all that. What's left?"' Matthew 19:16-18, 20-23, 25-26 (The Message)

To relate it to our analogy, the man could have been saying: 'How do I ride a big bike? I can see the life you are talking about, Jesus, and I want it too. I want to follow you, to ride alongside you, but my bike doesn't seem to be able to.'

Jesus' response would be something along the lines of: 'Ok, let me show you the basics — bum on seat, hands on handle bars, feet on the peddles, now cycle!' And the man says: 'I've done all that, what's left?'

Clearly the man knows he's missing something. He can feel a restriction on him, but he can't work out what it is. It would be like a child on a bike, watching his big brother going up and down all the curbs and gaining speed, and because of his little stabilisers, being unable to do the same.

Then Jesus says this:

'"If you want to give it all you've got," Jesus replied, "go sell your possessions; give everything to the poor. All your wealth will then be in heaven. Then come follow me." That was the last thing the young man expected to hear. And so, crest-fallen, he walked away. He was holding on tight to a lot of things, and he couldn't bear to let go.'

So now we see Jesus pinpoint the artificial stabiliser that was keeping the rich man's life upright, balanced, and moving forward in his own strength. His security, identity, and sense of power, worth and value, were all tied up in his riches; and Jesus asks him to let go, to sell his stuff, to take off the artificial stabilisers as it were, and to learn to ride the bike of his life by trusting Him.

Maybe for you it's not money; maybe it's a relationship, or an addiction, or a fear that you keep at bay by doing all the things you feel you should.

Whatever it is, whatever the reason is, if you are trying to follow Jesus, then you've got to learn to take off the stabilisers.

Whatever it is, whatever the reason is, if you are trying to follow Jesus, if you want to know the fullness and the freedom of the open road — no restrictions, no being held back — then you've got to learn to take off the stabilisers.

We need to come to a point where we can:

> 'Lean on, trust in, and be confident in the Lord with all your heart and mind and do not rely on your own insight or understanding.' Proverbs 3:5 (Amplified Version)

Artificial stabilisers cause us to lean on our own insight and understanding. And then when trouble comes our way; when we can't seem to hold it all together, when the things we have been leaning on get taken away, that's when our world can feel like it comes crashing down.

Caught in the arms of love

I remember when we were teaching our boys to ride bikes (when I say 'we', I mean 'he', my husband, as he did most of the legwork; I just took video footage!). Our boys were very reluctant to take the stabilisers off. And understandably so — fear was telling them that they could not manage to keep upright on only two wheels; fear was telling them that they would get hurt, that it wasn't safe to be so vulnerable.

Fear tells us exactly the same thing when we decide to give God a new level of trust. But in the same way that we gently explained to our children that their father would hold their bikes for them, that he would run alongside them and not let them fall, so God our Father tells us the same thing.

> 'Never will I leave you, never will I forsake you' (Joshua 1:5)

> 'Do not be afraid [of them] for I am with you and will rescue you,' declares the Lord.' (Jeremiah 1:8)

I have a memory of seeing my husband running alongside my son's bike, holding onto the back of the saddle, shouting instructions and encouragement in equal measure; when suddenly my little boy lost control of the bike. The steering wheel wobbled, he lost his balance, and the bike went hurtling towards the ditch at the side of the road. Within a split second, my husband let go of the saddle, and with a deft stroke, swooped my son into the safety of his father's arms. The bike went crashing down with a clatter and a bang, but no harm came to my son. He held on tight, and within moments, my husband had him back on his bike, trying again.

It's such a clear example of how God relates to us. When we choose to trust Him, when we take off those stabilisers and allow God to become our stabiliser, He will not let us down.

> **When we choose to trust Him, when we take off those stabilisers and allow God to become our stabiliser, He will not let us down.**

Yes, life may feel a little wobbly, we may lose our balance and feeling of control, but even if things come crashing down around us, He will lift us up into His loving arms. We have to come to a point where we stop saying to God: 'Prove it and I'll trust you'; and listen to Him say: 'Trust me and I'll prove it.'

In her book *The Hiding Place,*, Corrie ten Boom writes: 'Never be afraid to trust an unknown future to a known God.' In my journey of learning to trust God more and more, this simple sentence has been a frequent challenge.

> Psalm 9:10
> 'Those who know your name will trust in you, for you, Lord, have never forsaken those who seek you.'

'Those who *know* your name...' The way to trust is to know; know His character, know His heart towards you, know that He loves you, and that He is setting you up for success. He has no vested interest in watching you fail. He is not a God who throws his children into the fire to teach them that it is hot. He is trustworthy. His heart towards you is pure, and you can trust, rely and lean on him. There is no need for artificial stabilisers!

There's a well-known 'trust exercise' often used in team-building and personal development games, where you have to close your eyes and fall back into the arms of another person. I once used this example as part of a message I was preaching, and I needed to choose someone to stand behind me to catch me.

I scanned the auditorium looking for someone I could pick, and my eyes fell upon the front row, where my husband was sitting. Immediately, I asked him to come up and stand behind me, so that I could demonstrate the point. I closed my eyes, took a deep breath, and fell back. And of course, he caught me. The thing is, my level of fear at falling back was greatly reduced by choosing him to catch me. Why? Because I *know* him. I trust him, and I know that he would never let me fall.

When we get to know God intimately, our trust increases. When we discover His true intention towards us: 'to prosper and not to harm us, to give us hope and a future' (Jeremiah

29:11), and we choose to believe that, then we can begin to build trust in Him. This trust will lead us to be able to let go of the things we thought were protecting us — those walls we build up to guard our hearts — when in fact all those walls do is keep us isolated.

> Psalm 9:10
> 'Those who know your name will trust in you, for you, Lord, have never forsaken those who seek you.'

'For you, Lord, have never forsaken those who seek you.' If we want to know Him, we need to seek Him. Being willing to trust Him means that we need to be willing to seek Him. How can we know or trust Him if we have not bothered to find Him?

A few days ago, my teenage son asked me if I knew where the DVD that he wanted to watch with his friends was. I told him that I didn't know, and that he should look for it. He shrugged his shoulders and said that he'd given it a quick look, but hadn't found it. My reply was more profound than I realised or intended; I said: 'If you can't be bothered to look for it, then you don't want it enough!'

As soon as it came out of my mouth, I felt the Holy Spirit say: 'Amen!' Jeremiah 29:12-14 comes right after the famous promise of verse 11: 'I know the plans I have for you- plans to give you hope and a future. It says:

> 'Then you will call on me and come and pray to me, and I will listen to you. You will seek me and find me when you seek me with all your heart. I will be found by you,' declares the Lord, 'and will bring you back from captivity.'

The choice to trust Him, the choice to seek Him, and therefore get to know Him, are all key ingredients to living a life liberated from captivity.

The choice to trust Him, the choice to seek Him, and therefore get to know Him, are all key ingredients to living a life liberated from captivity; they are all nacre responses.

He is a God of 'instead'. He is the One who enables the very process of turning our pain into pearls. It's through a relationship of trust and faith in Him and His word that we are able to make an exchange, enter into a process that allows us to release a variety of nacre responses to whatever adversity we may be facing.

The following chapters will examine the various other nacre responses we can have that enable us, like the oyster, to turn any violation into a pearl of great value.

Chapter 3:

What You Tolerate, You'll Never Change

What you tolerate, you'll never change; the oyster knows this. The oyster has been given the ability to understand that a violation – a small parasite or grain of sand – cannot be tolerated. Tolerating it, ignoring it, and hoping it will go away in time will allow that violation to slowly corrupt the soft, fleshy part of the oyster; the part that gives it life.

Sometimes, I wonder if oysters have more sense than people! Just like the oyster, God has created us to respond. He has made us able to deal with a violation in any number of ways. But first, there has to be a decision that 'this' — whatever that is for you — is no longer acceptable.

There are many reasons why young women apply to Mercy Ministries: they want to see change in their lives; they want to see broken relationships restored; they want to experience happiness; to overcome depression; to beat addictions and destructive habits; to conquer an eating disorder; or to overcome their past. Each of these incredibly brave young women has taken a long hard look at her life and made the decision that her life must change.

The upside is that they are looking for God to make the changes that they need in order to be fulfilled; the 'bad news' (for them) is the realisation that God does not change lives — God changes *people,* and then those people change their lives.

Tolerance paralyses change.

Tolerance paralyses change. Unless we are prepared to do what it takes to arise within ourselves and say, 'No more!' we will continue to live in a cycle of destruction.

There's a story in Luke 8 about a woman with the issue of blood. She is one of my heroes. This woman had been bleeding for 12 years (a disgraceful disorder that carried immense shame and stigma in those times). She had plenty of opportunity to give up hope; to decide that this was her lot, this was all she could hope for — some meagre existence hiding away from the crowd — shamed, excluded, in pain, rejected, shunned and without means to live, having spent all she had on trying to get well.

She could have given in to despair, and yet something inside of her refused to give up. She had an inner strength; a spark of hope that refused to be extinguished. And so, on this particular day, she chose a nacre response. She had heard of Jesus' fame, of His ability to heal the sick, and instead of staying on her sick bed, her response was to rise up and push through.

She had to battle through the crowds who stood in her way; she faced rejection and ridicule from people she knew; she had to crawl on her hands and knees, and yet she refused to back down.

This woman reached out with all she had and touched the hem of his garment. Her breakthrough came, not because Jesus found her, but because *she* chose to rise up and find Jesus.

Her breakthrough came, not because Jesus found her, but because she chose to rise up and find Jesus.

In darkness, we rise

Proverbs 31:15 says this:

> 'She gets up whilst it's still dark; she provides food for her family and portions for her servant girls.'

I do not like mornings: fact. I'm terrible at getting up in the mornings. I genuinely believe that we shouldn't have to get out of bed until the sun says so! So when I read this scripture many years ago, I wanted to ignore it. In fact, for a long time I did ignore it, until one day I felt the Holy Spirit draw my attention to it. Again and again I read those words: '...she gets up whilst it's still dark', until suddenly I heard Him whisper: 'In other words, whilst darkness surrounds them, the people of God rise up.'

It totally changed my perspective on that verse. When darkness surrounds us, when circumstances tell us to stay down, to throw the duvet over our heads because we cannot face our lives, it's in those very moments that our response should be to rise up! That is a nacre response. Rising up is a response to difficulty that will instantly increase your chances of overcoming.

From Pain to Pearls

Imagine you were lying down on the floor. Your view and perspective would be severely restricted. You'd only be able to see the immediate surroundings. Your lying down posture would not give you the advantage of a long-distance view. The same is true when we are 'lying down' inside ourselves. When we refuse to rise up, we become completely overwhelmed with the immediate circumstances we are facing. The imminent job loss, the health scare, the difficult relationships all begin to consume our thinking; worry begins to gnaw away on the inside and before we know it, we're on a downward spiral.

Not only is your view restricted when you lie down, you will also find that your movement is restricted. When you are lying down, you can't move around much; there are few options for escape. Your defences are low because you are laid low. Not only that, but you are not in a position to help anyone.

Now imagine rising up on your feet. Immediately your perspective changes, immediately you are able to see your surroundings; you are able to see a way out when you stand up. Standing up also means you can move around because you are on your feet. Your eyes can see further and your feet can get you there. And what's more, a person who is standing up — a person who has risen up and changed their posture to a standing one — can reach down and help another up.

There is an immediate strength that comes from changing your physical posture. If you are feeling low right now — if you are feeling down, overwhelmed or ready to just give in, then be encouraged. Tell yourself it's time to rise up!

In fact, if that is how you are feeling right now, why don't you physically get down on the floor, and really think about the disadvantage, the exposure and vulnerable position this posture puts you in. Now choose to rise up. Make the effort to physically stand up on your feet and speak to yourself words of hope and encouragement.

Here are some scriptures to help you with this exercise:

> Isaiah 60:1 'ARISE' [from the depression and prostration in which circumstances have kept you; rise to a new life]!

> Psalm 20:8 'They are brought to their knees and fall, but we rise up and stand firm.'

> Exodus 14:13 'Do not be afraid. Stand firm and you will see the deliverance the LORD will bring you today.'

> 1 Corinthians 16:13 'Be on your guard; stand firm in the faith; be people of courage; be strong.'

> Galatians 5:1 'It is for freedom that Christ has set us free. Stand firm, then, and do not let yourselves be burdened again by a yoke of slavery.'

Believe and you will rise up

I know that some of you reading this will think that it's easy for me to write this when I have no idea of what you are facing. You may think that there is simply no way forward; no way to rise up when what you are facing is so beyond your strength and ability to endure. And you would be right;

I can't possibly know what you are going through right now,

but I do know that God is not asking you to rise up in your own strength.

Look at this man in John 5: 5-8:

> 'One of the men lying there had been sick for thirty-eight years. When Jesus saw him and knew he had been ill for a long time, he asked him, "Would you like to get well?"
>
> "I can't, sir," the sick man said, "for I have no one to put me into the pool when the water bubbles up. Someone else always gets there ahead of me." Jesus told him, "Stand up, pick up your mat, and walk!"' (New Living Translation)

I find it interesting that Jesus asked a man who had been sick for over three decades if he wanted to be well. Why did He ask him that? I believe it's because Jesus knew that this man would need to be at the point of no longer wanting to tolerate his condition in order for him to be healed.

We find excuses for our dysfunction and in doing so, create a space for it to exist.

You see, so often we blame everyone else. We blame our past, our hurts and our dysfunctions, as the reasons why we just can't quite make it up off the floor of our lives.

We find excuses for our dysfunction and in doing so, create a space for it to exist. Then Jesus comes along and offers us hope. He asks us if we want to get well. And often, like the man in the story did, we immediately give Jesus the reasons why we can't be well; why we can't rise up; why we will be the ones who are left behind yet again.

But Jesus knows that you are crippled. He knows that you've got good reason to still be sitting down waiting for your life to change; and yet He says the same thing to you and me that He said to that man 2000 years ago: 'Stand up, pick up your mat, and walk!'

We are never meant to try and get up in our own strength; all we need to do is be obedient to His Word. That crippled man had laid low for 38 years, and had every reason not to believe that Jesus' words could give him the power to rise up. The cripple didn't say: 'Heal me first and then I'll walk.' He simply believed and obeyed, and in his response to the Word of God, the miracle came.

When Jesus says, 'Stand up', He will give you the ability to do so.

If you feel you cannot rise up, that you simply have no strength of your own, that's ok. Jesus will give you what you need. All you need to do is believe, respond, and decide in your heart that when Jesus says, 'Stand up', He will give you the ability to do so.

Put on the armour, so you can stand

Rising up is one of the nacre responses we can have to life's adversities; we can choose to get up off the floor and take a

31

stand. Like the oyster, we can release something inside our heart and mind that enables us to position ourselves to not just survive, but to overcome.

> 'We are hard pressed on every side, yet not crushed; we are perplexed, but not in despair; persecuted, but not forsaken; struck down, but not destroyed' (2 Corinthians 4:8-9).

The fact is, like the loving Father He is, God has made it possible that even in the face of incredible pressures, we will not be defeated. We are able to stand up against everything the world has to throw at us and still emerge victorious.

How can we do this? The answer lies not in ourselves, but in a divine and unbeatable defense: the armour of God. God has given us His power and authority in the form of the Holy Spirit to work in and through us on a daily basis. Ephesians 6:10-12 encourages us to:

> 'Be strong in the Lord and in his mighty power. Put on the full armour of God so that you can take your stand against the devil's schemes.'

The devil has many schemes with regards to our walk with God. Fear, regret, unbelief, doubt, worry, depression, abuse, low self-esteem and worthlessness are all part of his plan to keep you separated from your destiny in God. The Bible says this:

> 'Be prepared. You're up against far more than you can handle on your own. Take all the help you can get, every weapon God has issued.' Ephesians 6:13 (The Message)

The very fact that the Bible is so clear about our armour and our defences against the schemes of the enemy is proof that, although we are not immune to struggle or duress, we can combat it. We are well equipped, like the oyster, to defend against attack.

Our spiritual lives and future in God's Kingdom are on the line. If we lose this war, we lose everything.

The devil is referred to in the Bible as being one who comes to 'steal, kill and destroy' (John 10:10) and that he is like a 'roaring lion, prowling around looking for someone to devour' (1 Peter 5:8). As in the animal kingdom, a lion will prey on the weak, so the devil preys on our weaknesses.

God has equipped us with the full armour we need for any form of action we need to take in our spiritual lives. In Ephesians 6, Paul sets the scene for us: we are fighting a war, and the stakes are higher than they have ever been in human history.

Faced with the cares of this world, we can easily forget about the severity of this battle. But make no mistake; our spiritual lives and future in God's Kingdom are on the line. If we lose this war, we lose everything. What can we do in the face of such overwhelming odds? Is there any hope?

Paul has the answer. In Ephesians 6:13, he gives the call to arms:

'Therefore, put on every piece of God's armour so you will be able to resist the enemy in the time of evil. Then after the battle you will still be standing firm. Stand your ground, putting on the belt of truth and the body armour of God's righteousness. For shoes, put on the peace that comes from the Good News so that you will be fully prepared. In addition to all of these, hold up the shield of faith to stop the fiery arrows of the devil. Put on salvation as your helmet, and take the sword of the Spirit, which is the word of God.'

These words were not written in the tranquil state of a life lived in pleasant circumstances. Every one of these words that the apostle Paul wrote was born out of his total conviction that the only way to respond to his circumstances (he was held captive in a cold, dark dungeon; tortured and ridiculed for his faith) was to rise up in the strength of what God has made available. By putting on all of God's armour, we can have a nacre response to the onslaught.

Jesus rose up amidst His darkness and in doing so, He conquered death and made a way for each of us to do the same.

When the apostle Paul chose to write this passage amidst the adversity of his situation, he allowed the Holy Spirit to use him in such a way that would affect the rest of us forevermore. His choice to rise up has meant that across the generations, we can learn from his words and actions and be encouraged. Every time you choose to apply the Word, to get armoured up, you inspire someone else to do the same.

Rising up for purpose

There is no shame in finding yourself in a dark place. We all experience times of feeling downtrodden with the weight of darkness around us. Jesus felt it too. In fact, He was down for three days. For three days He was surrounded by darkness. He had every opportunity to stay down, to give in to death and submit to the pain of His crucifixion. But He chose to rise up! Jesus rose up amidst His darkness and in doing so, He conquered death and made a way for each of us to do the same.

The fact is that rising up, like the Proverbs 31 woman we looked at earlier, is never just for our own benefit. Let's go back to that scripture:

> 'She gets up whilst it's still dark; she provides food for her family and portions for her servant girls.'

You see, this woman rose up for a purpose. Daylight was on its way, and she knew there would be mouths to feed. There are people on the other side of your breakthrough. There are those who are attached to your life right now who need you to rise up. Your staying down — your playing it safe — does not serve them well. Maybe you have children, and if you do, then their ability to deal with life and all its difficulties in the future, is heavily influenced by your ability in the present.

Darkness is your rising up time; it is your chance to learn the tools for overcoming adversity, because daylight will come. And when daylight comes, there will be many who need the lessons you've learnt and the tools you've applied, to be explained to them. We need to be those who learn lessons in life not just for our own benefit, but so that we can be carriers of truth, of hope, and of freedom.

From Pain to Pearls

Chapter 4: The *Nacre* of Forgiveness

Imagine your heart is like the oyster I have been describing. You are just going about your business in the deep blue ocean. You have a nice hard shell that is designed to keep you protected; but every now and again, something gets past your defences.

It could be the equivalent of a small grain of sand, or a vicious parasite intent on eating you from the inside out, or even a small shard of your own shell that dislodges. But before you know it, the very thing that was meant to protect you is causing you damage.

Now you find that your heart is at risk because something has got in there that you can't get out. You try and try to forget, you harden your outer shell, but it's too late: you got hurt; you were betrayed; she let you down; he caused you pain; you've been lied to, cheated on, abandoned, neglected and rejected; and now you have a choice to make – life or death?

The oyster's strategy of defending itself against something that has lodged within its core being, is probably one of the clearest metaphors God has ever given me regarding forgiveness.

We all live in an environment where the same grains of sand that can kill an oyster can make their way inside of us and begin to cause damage. For us, those grains of sand can be offence, neglect, betrayal, abuse, disappointment, sin, lies, adultery, grief, gossip … the list goes on.

37

The level of damage we sustain is not dependent on the severity of the offence; it is dependant on our response to it.

The fact is, life can be harsh and we will suffer some degree of hurt and pain along the way: it's inevitable. But the level of damage we sustain is not dependent on the severity of the offence; it is dependant on our response to it. We may not be able to choose what happens to us, but we can choose our response.

An oyster can be killed by only one small piece of sand or by a large parasite that eats it up. Either way, the end result is death on the inside and either way, the life-saving response is nacre; and one of the most vital nacre responses we can have is forgiveness. To choose not to forgive is to choose to allow the process of decay and erosion to slowly kill you from the inside out, when instead you could chose life, freedom and hope – all tied up in a thing called forgiveness.

Forgiveness is part of God's heart towards us. It's in His nature to forgive; His desire, in fact His *commandment,* is that we forgive also.

'Forgive and you will be forgiven.' Luke 6:37

God's forgiveness towards us is intertwined with our forgiveness of others.

This is why without forgiveness, true freedom is impossible to attain. Unforgiveness opens a doorway for bitterness, anger, regret, pain and hatred to take up residence in our heart and begin to eat us up from the inside out, like a parasite. This is why the enemy has twisted, corrupted, and shrouded in lies and half-truths the concept of forgiveness; in an attempt to mask the power that forgiveness has to set us free.

Forgiveness is the mechanism whereby we say: 'It's not okay what you did, but the judgement of your behaviour belongs to God, not to me.'

Let's look at some of the lies and misconceptions we can have about forgiveness and address each one:

'If I forgive, it will feel like I am condoning what happened'

Sometimes we resist forgiveness because it can feel as if we are condoning the behaviour, making it seem like we are accepting what has happened to us as okay. But forgiveness is not about those who have hurt you: it's about you. As we acknowledge unforgiveness and look at the full impact of our hurt, we can work through the painful memories and reach a place of forgiveness. There are no shortcuts. Pretending would only sabotage true healing.

Forgiveness is the mechanism whereby we say: 'It's not okay what you did, but the judgement of your behaviour belongs to God, not to me.' Forgiveness fully accepts and acknowledges

39

the hurt and pain that has been caused; it does not belittle it, nor does it justify the behaviour of those who hurt you. What has been done to you is a debt of sin, and all sin is against God. So when you forgive, you are transferring the debt of sin from your 'accounts ledger' to God's, leaving the judging for Him to do. Forgiveness equals freedom from a burden that is not yours to carry.

Romans 12:19 states:

> 'Don't insist on getting even; that's not for you to do.
> "I'll do the judging", says God. "I'll take care of it."'
> (The Message)

'I will never be able to forget what happened, so how can I forgive it?'

God asks us to forgive, not forget. Even if we could, it wouldn't be wise to erase from our memory all the wrongs done to us and by us. If we did, we would never learn from our experiences and would be caught in a perpetual cycle of reliving the same situations, fears, disappointments and abuse. However, what can be healed — and is in fact one of the things that forgiveness releases — is the damaging effect of the raw emotions associated with the events.

As we commit to releasing this nacre of forgiveness, the sharp edges of that violation or offense are covered to the point where they can cause no more damage and it ceases to hurt. So whilst we may not be able to forget, we can choose to forgive, and in doing so, embrace an opportunity for the pain caused by those events to be healed forever. Forgiveness takes the sting out of the memory; it embraces healing, and in so doing, it allows us to turn what the enemy meant for evil into good (Gen 50:20).

Forgiveness is not earned — trust is.

If I forgive them, do I have to trust them?

Forgiving someone is an act of your obedience given by you whether the other person has asked for your forgiveness or not. Forgiveness is not earned — trust is. We are not expected to blindly trust someone who has hurt us. That is both naïve and irresponsible! If a person steals, you wouldn't give him a key to your house. If they gossip, you'd be foolish to trust them with your secrets. As such, forgiving a wrong does not mean extending the person an invitation to sin again.

You see, forgiveness isn't the same as reconciliation. Yes, forgiveness is the start of reconciliation, but reconciliation isn't always the goal of forgiveness. In fact, as I just pointed out, there are situations where reconciliation is not a good idea. If the other person is unwilling to change or is unwilling to reconcile, then you can still forgive, but it's not necessary to seek reconciliation when the other person is unrepentant, unchanging, unwilling or unsafe for you.

'I don't feel very forgiving'

Forgiveness starts with a decision; but it is more than simply deciding. Forgiveness is a choice to begin a process that may take time. Forgiveness rarely comes from feelings. In fact, our

41

feelings will often work against us during the process of forgiveness.

Your feelings may tell you that forgiving is weak; that there is a kind of protective power in your anger and resentment towards that person; that somehow your bitterness against them keeps you separate and protected from them.

In fact, the very opposite is true; your unforgiveness actually ties you to them, spiritually and emotionally. Imagine a long piece of elastic tied to your life and to the lives of every single person you have unforgiveness towards. Try as you may to move on, to forget, to put aside the memories and bury them somewhere within yourself; you will simply take two steps forward, strain at the elastic, and it will ping you right back to where you started. The rawness and emotions of what hurt you will never be healed without snipping that elastic.

So, there is only one solution — a pair of scissors called forgiveness. Each choice you make to forgive from the heart, each release of nacre if you like, snips one of the cords; and before you know it, you will be free.

Forgiveness requires an act of your will: an act of obedience to God's will, and if you ask Him to help you, I can guarantee you He will! Right feelings follow right actions; and as you act on the decision to forgive, the feelings will eventually follow.

'Do I just forgive the 'big' things?'

Forgiveness is not something you do just to be free from your past — forgiveness is a way of life. People will hurt you, upset you, overlook you and let you down. You will make mistakes and you will let others down; and forgiveness is the nacre that flows through your life to keep each of those 'ouch' moments from being the start of a deeper root. So, whilst forgiving the 'big' things is all good and well, it's actually the day-to-day walking in forgiveness that protects us.

Like I said, forgiveness is like a pair of scissors — it's a tool; and therefore it will always be what you use to cut something. Whether you are a small child learning to use scissors for the first time, or whether you are an 'expert' scissor user, whenever you need to cut something, a pair of scissors is what you'll go for.

The tool doesn't change just because you are now proficient in using it. There is no 'higher level' where forgiveness stops being something that you need. You don't graduate past the use of scissors; you just become more adept at using them!

'I have forgiven everyone else, but I can't forgive myself'

The detrimental effect of unforgiveness is not dependent on who the unforgiveness is aimed at. As I already mentioned, unforgiveness keeps that elastic band tight between you and the trauma of what you are trying to forgive. The damage that unforgiveness causes inside of us is no less when the unforgiveness is directed at ourselves. You will still be unable to move forward — unable to receive healing and freedom from whatever is causing you pain on the inside — whilst ever you hold unforgiveness towards anyone, including yourself and even God. Even though God has not done you harm, if your perception of Him is that He has let you down or disappointed you, don't be afraid to tell Him that.

Perception is reality: if you believe God has let you down or caused you pain, respond to that perception with forgiveness. Regardless of the fact that God's ways are higher than ours, and we may never understand certain situations, just trying to be a 'nice Christian' by pretending that you are okay with God will not help you. You need to know that He is well able to handle every ounce of your darkest emotions towards Him; and once it's all out, your choice to forgive Him will help you be able to hear what He has to say for Himself.

Forgiveness is nacre. It smoothes the edges off the pain; it cools the heat of hatred; it takes the sting out of bitterness.

When you open up your lines of communication with Him and tell Him how you really feel, you will find that God Himself will speak into your heart and into your situation in such a way that brings healing and restoration. The choice to forgive is the very beginning of that process of healing.

Forgiveness is nacre. It smoothes the edges off the pain; it cools the heat of hatred; it takes the sting out of bitterness. This nacre will turn your pain into a pearl of great value and bring you life — if you let it!

Having written this, I must add that revelation isn't transformation. Just because you may now have a greater understanding of forgiveness does not mean you are free or that you have forgiven. I may have given you a pair of scissors and described its purpose as a tool; but until you actually take hold of those scissors and snip those cords away, you will only know the purpose of forgiveness without feeling its benefits.

So here's what you can do — you can stop and ask the Holy Spirit to help you begin the process of forgiveness right now; you can choose to pray and to begin releasing that nacre, that flow of forgiveness towards those who have hurt you.

Prayer:

Father, I come before you now and ask that you would help me to forgive. Help me to be free from all that has happened to me: all the pain, the despair and the tormenting thoughts that go round and round.

Lord, I pray that you would make a way where there seems to be no way. I declare that each time I release forgiveness, the cords that have bound me will be broken. I choose to forgive all those who have played a part in the pain that I feel. I forgive --------------------- for -------------------.(list the names of those you need to forgive and what you are forgiving them for, include yourself if need be).

I release forgiveness, like nacre, in the Name of Jesus. I cut off any soul ties that bind me to the people that hurt me, I release them from their debt to me and place them in Your hands. I declare that this act of my will and obedience will produce in me a pearl of great value, a heart that is free and wounds that are healed.

In Jesus' name, Amen.

From Pain to Pearls

Chapter 5: Bah, Humbug

We all know the classic tale of Ebenezer Scrooge — the epitome of selfishness — the quintessential mean-spirited, miserly, narcissistic old man. However, as this timeless Charles Dickens story unfolds, it becomes clear that there are reasons for Scrooge's miserable approach to life.

When the Ghost of Christmas past comes to visit Scrooge, we catch a glimpse of his pain. His mother had died when he was only a baby and as a result, his father became depressed, leaving Scrooge to fend for himself on the streets. I remember watching the scene in the latest version of the movie, *A Christmas Carol* (2009), where we see Scrooge as a small boy, abandoned and forgotten in a dark, cold, Victorian classroom to celebrate Christmas alone.

Later, the ghost shows Scrooge how his success in business has made him become obsessive, developing a workaholic tendency. His money and work-obsessed personality traits eventually drive Scrooge's fiancée, Belle, to leave him, further hardening his heart. Finally, after Scrooge loses his sister, Fan, while she gives birth to his nephew, Scrooge loses all of his love for humanity; for life in general. He becomes a hard shell of a man with virtually no life left inside of him.

This is what life can be like for many of us: it's not just one thing that gets us, it's one thing after another; and before we know it, we become so overrun with memories, experiences and the consequences of our own bad choices, that we simply shut down and fail to respond to that grain of sand, the parasite, or the broken shell that is eroding our life away.

It's not until Ebenezer Scrooge is presented with his future; with a life that has produced nothing of value, no pearl from all that pain, that he decides to change his ways. And what nacre response does he have? Generosity and kindness! When he wakes up to find he's been given another chance, he becomes a model of kindness and generosity towards all those around him.

As the final narration states:

> *'Scrooge was better than his word. He did it all, and infinitely more; and to Tiny Tim, who did not die, he was a second father. He became as good a friend, as good a master, and as good a man, as the good old city knew, or any other good old city, town, or borough, in the good old world ... His own heart laughed: and that was quite enough for him.'*

Scrooge was not just generous with his money, but generous with his heart. He gave people time, he smiled, and he became a good friend and mentor. His kindness transformed those around him; but more than that, it transformed his own heart. Where the pain of his past had left him mean-spirited, and dead to life's pleasures, the nacre response of generosity left him laughing on the inside!

God chose generosity

'But to our wounds only God's wounds can speak; and not a god has wounds but Thou alone...' Edward Shillito

Has it ever occurred to you how much loss God the Father has suffered? I mean He lost what some would call His worship leader, the Archangel Lucifer, and with him, lost a third of the angelic host. Then God lost humanity; and because He'd given Adam and Eve dominion over the earth, He lost that too.

God's own response to loss was to give!

Don't for a second believe that God did not feel the pain and disappointment of those losses. Knowing ahead of time that they would happen does not lessen their impact.

What this shows me so strengthens my love and respect for our heavenly Father: that He would not ask me to do something He wouldn't do Himself. He too has had to choose a response to pain. He too has had to release nacre, as it were; and the nacre He chose was generosity. God's own response to loss was to give!

> 'For God so loved the world that he gave his one and only Son, that whoever believes in him shall not perish but have eternal life.' (John 3:16)

Out of the myriad of responses to pain and loss that God Almighty could have used, He chose the one that would save us all. His generosity, His heart to reconcile and be in relationship with us caused Him to give His only Son.

And even in His generosity there was suffering. This short extract from *The Cross of Christ* by John R.W. Stott illustrates this beautifully:

> 'In the real world of pain, how could one worship a God who was immune to it? I have entered many Buddhist temples in different Asian countries and stood respectfully before the statue of the Buddha, his legs crossed, arms folded, eyes closed, the ghost of a smile

playing round his mouth, a remote look on his face, detached from the agonies of the world. But each time, after a while I have had to look away.

And in imagination I have turned instead to the lonely, twisted, tortured figure on the cross, nails through hands and feet, back lacerated, limbs wrenched, brow bleeding from thorn pricks, mouth dry and intolerably thirsty, plunged in God-forsaken darkness. That is the God for me! He laid aside His immunity to pain. He entered our world of flesh and blood, tears and death. He suffered for us.

Our sufferings become more manageable in the light of His. There is still a question mark against human suffering, but over it we stamp another mark, the cross which symbolizes divine suffering.'

God responded to His personal loss with a personal gift, for the greater good. God's pain resulted in the greatest pearl ever produced: Jesus Christ. And the nacre response of generosity is what made that possible. That spirit of generosity lives in each of us. Generosity is God's own heartbeat; it's His nature. And as we have been made in His image (Genesis 1:26), we also have received that nature.

A recent study, found in the journal *Nature* [David G. Rand, Joshua D. Greene and Martin A. Nowak], proves this to be true. It found that people seemed to be inherently more generous than selfish: that generosity is an innate response, but that given time, we can reason our way to a more selfish decision.

In the study, researchers ran several tests in which each participant in a small group received money and then had to decide how much to invest in a shared group fund. The more time people had to choose how much to donate, the less they gave.

Furthermore, subjects who were told they had to make a decision within 10 seconds gave more than others who were told they had to wait the same 10 seconds before deciding. Because snap decisions are based on intuition, the researchers concluded that generosity is the intuitive human response.

God's pain resulted in the greatest pearl ever produced: Jesus Christ.

This is what God says about the importance of choosing generosity as a nacre response to pain and adversity:

> 'Don't hit back; discover beauty in everyone. If you've got it in you, get along with everybody. Don't insist on getting even; that's not for you to do. "I'll do the judging," says God. "I'll take care of it." Our Scriptures tell us that if you see your enemy hungry, go buy that person lunch, or if he's thirsty, get him a drink. Your generosity will surprise him with goodness. Don't let evil get the best of you; get the best of evil by doing good.' Romans 12:19-21 (The Message)

So what do I mean about generosity being nacre? How can we be expected to respond with generosity at a time when we may feel we have nothing to give, or we simply don't want to give because we have shut ourselves down in our attempt at self-preservation?

It seems, somehow, that when we repay evil with good, we gain a victory over it. In other words, when we choose to respond in the midst of our own lack with a generous spirit, we take the enemy by surprise, and are able to coat the destructive effects of whatever adversity we are facing with a nacre that transforms those effects into a stunning pearl of value. It's not easy by any means, but it is worth it.

My friend tells of a time in her life when God asked her to go and pray for a couple who came forward in church for prayer for infertility: just when she had learned that her own treatment had failed again. She had to see beyond her own pain and disappointment and choose the nacre response of generosity. She sowed a seed: she gave a gift of faith and prayer when she so needed it herself. She has two babies of her own now.

Another friend ran a Bible study with some young women along the theme of love and marriage at a time when her husband had just confessed to an affair, and they were desperately trying to rebuild their own marriage. Rising above her own disillusionment, her own sense of betrayal, she chose the nacre response of generosity. She gave of her time; she opened her home and sowed seeds of hope and strength into others when she needed it for herself. Their marriage is now stronger than ever.

When my newborn nephew was diagnosed with congenital hypoplastic left heart syndrome, and given only a small chance of surviving his first set of operations, I immediately set up a standing order with the British Heart Foundation. Why? Not because doing so would increase his chances of survival, that's just silly superstition. No, I did it because I wanted my response to this painful experience to be one of generosity. Giving to that charity is my way of saying to the enemy: 'You will not stifle me; you will not corrode me on the inside with fear and sadness. I will give faithfully into a charity that stands for healing and for research; and in years to come, it may be the very organisation that discovers a way to fix his heart permanently.' (We are of course also praying for miraculous healing!)

Kindness and generosity amidst the carnage

Humanity is at its most divine when we show kindness amidst carnage. When amidst our own fear and pain we respond from a place of generosity and kindness, we send a message of hope that lifts the spirit and softens our hearts and in so doing, we reveal our origins as being made in the image of a good God.

Out of the horror of the Boston marathon bombings (April 15 2013), there emerged story after story of human kindness, as the city's residents did all they could to help those caught up in the attack. I remember watching the images unfold and seeing many of those closest to the bombsite run towards the disaster, not away from it.

One of the most shared messages on Twitter was a quote from American television host and Presbyterian minister, Fred Rogers: 'Look for the helpers. You'll always find people who are helping.' And it proved to be true.

In a rush to donate blood, so many of the runners continued to run across the finishing line and onwards to the Massachusetts General Hospital, that they had to be turned away. People opened their homes, people carried the injured; and anonymous bystanders began to direct the traffic, as police resources became over-stretched. Restaurants in the area offered free meals and shelter to those caught up in the tragedy, allowing people to pay only if they were able to.

When we respond to tragedy and loss with a heart full of kindness and generosity, it releases nacre.

One of the tweets I came across said this: 'Come for open wifi, place to charge your phone, cold drinks, or just don't want to be alone'. It came from the owner of El Pelon, a Mexican restaurant in the area nearest the bombing. Later, in an interview, he said: 'My coworkers and staff deserve a lot of credit: not one blinked when asked, not one went home when they could, and those not working came in.' Even in giving praise to his staff team, he showed a generous spirit.

Whether it's on a large scale like the Boston bombings or in the everyday challenges of life, when we respond to tragedy and loss with a heart full of kindness and generosity, it releases nacre. This nacre coats the pain of that trauma with the hope that amidst it all, we brought some relief, some joy to another human being.

The Bible puts it like this in 2 Corinthians 8:2:

> 'In spite of their terrible ordeal of suffering, their abundant joy and deep poverty have led them to be abundantly generous.' (International Standard Version)

Pain and suffering does not have to lead us to misery and brokenness. We may not be able to control what happens to us, but we can control our response to it. When we choose generosity and kindness towards another's pain and tragedy, it miraculously takes an edge off our own. It becomes part of our healing, part of our ability to overcome, and in it all we become just a little more like Jesus.

From Pain to Pearls

Chapter 6: Where Is Your 'There'?

Driven to distraction

The garden needs watering, so I turn on the hose and as I do so, I look over at my car and notice it needs washing. As I go into the house to get the things I need to clean the car, I notice the postman has been and so I decide to go through the post. I pick up the post, put my car keys on the side, separate out the bills that need paying and throw the junk mail in the rubbish bin in the kitchen, and notice that it is full.

So, I decide to put the bills back on the side and take out the rubbish first, as it is bin day today. But then I think, since I'm going to be near the post-box when I put the bins out on the street, I may as well pay the bills first.

I go find my cheque-book in the downstairs study, and see that there is only one cheque left. My extra cheques are in the drawer upstairs, so I go to the drawer where I find the can of Coke I'd been drinking earlier. I'm going to look for my cheques, but first I need to move the Coke aside so that I don't accidentally knock it over – that would be typical!

The Coke is getting warm, and I decide to put it in the fridge to keep it cold. As I head back downstairs toward the kitchen with the Coke, a vase of flowers in the living room catches my eye: they need water.

I put the Coke down by the vase and discover my sunglasses that I'd been looking for yesterday. I decide I better put them back in my handbag but first I'm going to water the flowers. I

57

set the glasses back down on the side, go to the kitchen and fill a container with water and suddenly spot the TV remote control. Those kids just leave everything lying around!

I know all too well that tonight when we watch TV, they will ask me where it is and I'll end up being the one looking for the remote control, but I won't remember where I last saw it! So I pick up the remote control to put it back where it belongs, but first I'll water the flowers.

I try to pour some water in the flowers, but the jug is cracked so most of it spills on the floor. I set the remote control on the side, get some towels and wipe up the spill. Then, I head down the hall trying to remember what I was planning to do.

Distractions and diversions are a common occurrence during times of trial and adversity.

At the end of the day, the garden isn't watered, the car isn't washed, the bills aren't paid, there is a can of warm Coke sitting next to the flowers that still only have a little bit of water, no one can find the remote control and when they ask me, I know I've seen it somewhere along with the sun-glasses I couldn't find. I also can't find my car keys. Then, when I try to figure out why nothing got done today, I'm really baffled because I know I was busy all day, and I'm really tired. I realise I have a serious problem, and I'll try to get some help for it, but first I have to check my emails!

Clearly this story isn't entirely true, nor is it serious in its nature. But there is a serious message in it. The fact is, distractions and diversions are a common occurrence during times of trial and adversity.

Sometimes we can't seem to concentrate; we can't quite get ourselves together. We can feel overwhelmed by the situation we find ourselves in and the fact that we know we're supposed to have some sort of response to it. There can be such a constant stream of problem-solving techniques, self-help manuals and to-do lists thrown at us, that we become completely ineffective in even making it through the day. And yet we feel exhausted by the sheer demand of the pressure our circumstances have placed on us.

The world we live in makes distraction really, really easy. The iPhone has an app for that, I'm sure! In my family, we've had to create 'device free' times and spaces to ensure we actually give care and attention to each other, instead of always disappearing into a virtual world of diversion and distraction.

In times of trouble, pain or adversity it is vital we are able to withdraw from the demands of whatever we are facing and connect to God's presence. There is a need to pray, to seek His face, to draw close to Him and to spend time with Him. We need to find stillness amidst the distraction and diversions of daily life.

When we consider oysters, the releasing of nacre in order to create a pearl from its pain is done internally. It is achieved in the secret place, away from public view; and so it is for us.

When the storms of life hit, when we are threatened by a free-fall into chaos, we need to find the eye of the storm.

When the storms of life hit, when we are threatened by a free-fall into chaos, we need to find the eye of the storm, the stillness amidst the rage, and there in that place, connect to the source of our strength, which comes from our intimacy with God.

The power of the secret place

Throughout the New Testament there are many examples of Jesus removing Himself from the crowd, to find the secret place. The demands, the distractions and diversions of the people's needs was not something He was prepared to face without building in time with His Father. He was fully aware that His environment was hostile, and unless He could respond to His external adversity with a nacre response, He would surely fail.

Luke 5:16 tells us that Jesus, '...often withdrew into the wilderness and prayed.' Jesus clearly valued and needed His time alone with Father God. He 'often withdrew', showing intent and deliberate action; Jesus made a choice to find the secret place.

A few years ago, I really felt a sense that God was asking me to draw closer to Him; to withdraw, as it were.

I had up until then lived along the same lines as Smith Wigglesworth's famous quote says: *'Rarely do I pray for an hour, but rarely does an hour go by when I do not pray'*. I had learned to pray quickly and often; on the go, in the moment. And there is nothing wrong with that – I still pray like that. But God wanted me to add something more to our relationship; a deepening of our intimacy.

The demands of my life were such that I simply could not find the time to 'hang out' with God. I would pray, petition and intercede mainly about the things He had given me to carry; I was preparing messages to speak, doing research for a book – all valuable 'spiritual' past-times, but the opportunity to recuperate and enjoy His presence was at the bottom of the list and I was constantly distracted from just spending time with Him.

And then we got a dog. Not my idea! I didn't want a dog. But we love our son, and his earnest request for a puppy, accompanied by heartfelt promises of walking, feeding and taking care of the dog, meant we gave in. That dog changed my life, because guess who takes that dog for walks every day? No, not my son, who made promises he failed to keep, but me. I am the one who walks every day, alone, in the rain, the snow, the wind and the occasional sunny day we have in Yorkshire. There is no computer; I turn my phone off and I listen to the sound of the trees. I smell the fresh air and I enjoy His presence. We chat. I talk, and then He talks and I listen.

That dog has made me send away the multitudes, like Jesus did in Matthew 14:23 so that He could be alone to pray:

> 'And when He had sent the multitudes away, He went up on the mountain by Himself to pray. Now when

evening came, He was alone there.'

Walking the dog, is my 'there' … where is yours? We all need to have the wisdom to send away our multitudes, our distractions and diversions and find our 'there', our place of quiet devotion, where we don't just pray our worries and hope we are heard, but where we are silent long enough to hear the answer.

Luke 6:12-13 tells us of one occasion when Jesus took all night to talk to God about an issue He was facing:

> 'Now it came to pass in those days that He went out to the mountain to pray, and continued all night in prayer to God. And when it was day, He called His disciples to Himself; and from them He chose twelve whom He also named apostles.'

Jesus spent long enough in prayer and conversation with God that He was able to discern what the Father's will was in regards to naming the apostles.

Jesus highly valued His intimacy with the Father. When it came to His hour of greatest testing, of pain beyond any He had ever endured, when He needed to find a nacre response to coat the pain, He went to His secret place and prayed. In the garden of Gethsemane (John 17), Jesus pours out His heart in prayer and there, in His secret place, God gives Him the grace to carry on. Despite His fear and doubt, Jesus was able to release a nacre response called prayer and devotion, and in communion with God was able to turn the pain of a crucifixion into the greatest pearl ever produced: the salvation of all mankind.

Shifting the focus

When we make it a priority to find the eye of the storm, to retreat from the multitudes and in the face of our adversity seek His face, it may not have an immediate impact on our circumstances and the situations we are facing, but it will certainly change the way we see them.

When Jesus cried out to God in the Garden of Gethsemane, His situation did not change; God did not remove the burden of the situation by changing the situation. God removed the burden of the situation by strengthening Jesus with the grace He needed to be able to go through with it.

We must choose to start speaking out the truth of God's Word, and choose to get to know Him more, especially through life's challenges.

Matthew 6:6 makes it clear:

> 'Here's what I want you to do: Find a quiet, secluded place so you won't be tempted to role-play before God. Just be there as simply and honestly as you can manage. The focus will shift from you to God, and you will begin to sense his grace.' (The Message)

Life's circumstances can and will conspire against us to keep us far from Him, distrusting His intentions and fearing the future. We must choose to start speaking out the truth of God's Word,

63

and choose to get to know Him more, especially through life's challenges. We need to know that He is not the source of our pain, so He can be the resource for our healing.

Paul the apostle knew this and lived by it, as evidenced by Philippians 4:11-13:

> 'I have learned to be content whatever the circumstances. I know what it is to be in need, and I know what it is to have plenty. I have learned the secret of being content in any and every situation, whether well fed or hungry, whether living in plenty or in want. I can do everything through him who gives me strength.'

He goes on to say:

> 'Do not fret or have any anxiety about anything, but in every circumstance and in everything, by prayer and definite requests, with thanksgiving, continue to make your wants known to God. And God's peace shall be yours, that tranquil state of a soul assured of its salvation through Christ, and so fearing nothing from God and being content with its earthly lot of whatever sort that is, that peace which transcends all understanding shall garrison and mount guard over your hearts and minds in Christ Jesus.'

We need to be those who respond to our pain and trouble with the nacre of prayer. We pray until things change, we pray until we see it. As believers, we can see in the spiritual, which gives us faith to keep praying until we see it in the natural. We pray with all kinds of prayers until peace comes, and according to this scripture above, peace can come despite the circumstances remaining the same.

doubt and fear that can be caused by the unpredictability of life's circumstances. According to God's promise in Philippians 4, when we pour out our hearts in prayer and thanksgiving, the peace of God mounts a garrison around our hearts and our minds. His peace stands guard and protects our inner being. It stops fear and anxiety from gnawing away on the inside of us and coats our circumstances with a nacre called peace that will protect us from every sharp edge and every destructive assault and releases us to find a calm in any storm.

From Pain to Pearls

Chapter 7:

A Banquet In The Presence Of Your Enemies

I don't like it when doctors say: 'hmmm,' with a concerned frown and a sideways tilt of the head that confirms your own concern wasn't just over-active imagination. A few years ago, this happened to me. The doctor frowned that frown and said 'hmmm' before telling me that the lump I had found would indeed need further investigation and she was sending me to the clinic the following day.

I went to the clinic and had a scan and a few hours later a different doctor did the same 'hmmmm' and the same frown as he looked at my results and told me that the lump they scanned was fine but that they'd found another that was of more concern. He said I would need a biopsy and that I could wait and have it done straight away. Once I had that biopsy, they told me I would need to wait around 10 days to find out if the lump was cancerous. There was around a 50% chance either way.

Within seconds of hearing the word 'cancer', my mind went into overdrive. Fear like I'd never felt before rose up inside me as I imagined my husband without his wife and my children without their mother. Seemingly, without permission and even without there being an actual diagnosis, I already had images of my funeral, images of my family's loss and a deep sense of panic as I wondered whether I was going to have to fight for my life.

But it wasn't my life I was about to fight for; it was my mind and my emotions. Those 10 days of waiting became for me a battle-ground; an opportunity to choose my response even before I knew which path this situation was going to take me down. It was as if a parasite called fear had just crawled past my outer shell and into the soft, fleshy part within me and now I had to choose a response.

I was presented with a choice: choose to produce nacre and stop the fear parasite gnawing away at me, or choose to set myself up for failure by passively submitting to this situation without any healthy internal response to the invasion of fear.

So I made my choice. I chose to turn to my Bible, one of the most important nacre responses to whatever life may throw at you. Jesus tells us in John 8:32 that the truth will set you free. This is a commonly quoted scripture but often without the context. Jesus actually says: 'And you shall know the truth and the truth will set you free.'

It's not the truth that sets you free; it's the truth you know that sets you free.

It's not the truth that sets you free; it's the truth you *know* that sets you free. And how else will you know the truth than to read the source of truth: the Word of God? Being able to respond to the trials and adversities of life from a godly perspective, means we need to develop a love for God's Word during good times and bad. The wise person builds their life on the rock; the unmovable foundation of truth their Maker spoke before they were even born.

I for one want to know what He has to say about what I find myself facing. I don't want to be one who seems to have my life all together until a storm hits, and it becomes clear that whilst the house looked as it should, the foundations were built on the shifting sands of circumstance and faulty belief systems.

Reading His Word has been a love of mine since I was a child, and so over time it's become a foundation which, when storms hit my life, though they may strip everything I've built away, provides me with the foundational truths of who I am and who He is to me.

The Word of God: His promises, His belief in us, His character and His plans and purposes for our lives, are found within the books of the Bible. Knowing and believing these things is essential to giving us the ability to turn simple words on a page into life-giving, faith-building, wisdom-growing nacre responses.

Imagine if I were to spill liquid on the floor. I could mop it up with newspaper or kitchen towels. Whilst the newspaper may be similar in composition to the kitchen towels, it only has a limited ability to absorb the liquid. It won't clean up the spill. The kitchen towel on the other hand absorbs every ounce of liquid, and carries it within itself. For me, learning to absorb the Word of God into the very core of what I believe about me, about Him and about life, has been the bedrock of strength that has seen me stand through many storms.

Picking up the story I began this chapter with, as I fought the battle for my mind, I decided to start with God's Word. I turned to Psalm 23, and verse 5 just grabbed me: 'You prepare a banquet before me in the presence of my enemies'. The situation I was facing felt hostile, and I felt the presence of my enemies, particularly fear. Yet here in God's Word He was promising to prepare a banquet for me. It was late at night and I was about to go to sleep, so I meditated on this scripture and as I drifted away I remember asking the Holy Spirit to explain to me why the banquet was in the presence of my enemies. What followed was the most powerful dream I've ever had.

By invitation only

In my dream I saw myself sitting at a large round dining table in a restaurant that I knew well. Around the table were my companions: Faith, Hope, Love, Joy, Peace, Wisdom and Strength. We chatted, laughed and sang together like the good friends we were. The scene was one of joy, fellowship and friendship.

As I watched the scene, I became aware of three figures who stood over in the shadows by the bar area. I wondered who they were and felt the Spirit of God tell me that they were my enemies: Fear, Worry and Unbelief. These enemies stared at me with such hatred, that it sent a cold ripple through my body. I asked God: 'Why are they here? They don't belong in this place.'

And He answered me: 'This restaurant, like your life, is open to the public. Life on earth is an open space that can sometimes be visited by enemies. But who sits at your table is by invitation only.' Even in my dream the truth of that statement hit me like a missile.

As I continued to observe the scene I saw myself become distracted by the figures at the bar. Each time I would steal a glance in their direction or cease the conversation with my companions, I could see them move towards me, until finally

Fear stood directly behind the seat of Faith and the entire scene stopped still. Everyone went quiet, the tension palpable in the air as both Fear and Faith looked me directly in the eyes.

And then I heard the voice of God: 'There are no more seats at your table and Faith will not share her seat with Fear: choose your companions wisely.'

Faith is a powerful weapon.

I woke up and realised the battle I faced would be won or lost in my mind before it ever hit my body. Faith is a powerful weapon and the first thing the enemy will try to do is separate us from the companions God has given to do our thought life with.

> 'The world is unprincipled. It's dog-eat-dog out there! The world doesn't fight fair. But we don't live or fight our battles that way—never have and never will.
>
> We use our powerful God-tools for smashing warped philosophies, tearing down barriers erected against the truth of God, fitting every loose thought and emotion and impulse into the structure of life shaped by Christ.
>
> Our tools are ready at hand for clearing the ground of every obstruction and building lives of obedience into maturity.' 2 Corinthians 10:4-6 (The Message)

In other words, we cannot control what goes on outside of us but we certainly can and should control what goes on, on the inside. The companions we engage with in our thought life will determine where our enemies are positioned. Taking every thought captive and making it obedient to Christ may be simple, but it isn't easy. It requires commitment, dedication and an assertive resolve to choose to believe what God says about you and the situation you face, rather than what your thoughts, feelings and facts may lead you to believe.

Taking every thought captive and making it obedient to Christ may be simple, but it isn't easy.

My nacre response to this particular situation was to ask the Holy Spirit to lead me to specific scriptures that were mine for what I was facing. What did He have to tell me about my health and my future? He gave me various key scriptures that became my anchor; they became what I tied myself to and any thought that did not line up with the truth of those scriptures I took hold of and subjected them to the truth of Jesus Christ.

It was simple but not easy. I became worn out by trying to fight my thoughts with more thoughts. It wasn't until I heard a preacher speak about the power of the spoken word that I began to see where I was going wrong. My nacre response to renew my mind and take every thought captive was correct but incomplete.

Let me explain it this way, by means of a little experiment. When you have a moment, begin to count to 10 in your head. Then, at a random point during the counting in your head, say your name out loud.

You will find that the counting in your head stops as soon as you engage your mouth and voice and speak your name. The thing is, you cannot fight thoughts with thoughts, you have to fight thoughts with words.

Whatever situation you may be facing, regardless of the level of trauma you may be experiencing, in order to respond with a nacre that will save you from destruction inside, you must engage your voice and take your thoughts captive. You must choose who you do your thought life with and verbally evict the enemies that loiter around your table in the fringes of your mind.

Here are some examples of common thoughts and belief statements that can erode like a parasite the soft tissue of your heart and leave nothing but an empty shell behind.

After each statement is the truth, based on God's Word, that becomes a weapon with which you fight. You can speak and declare this truth and demand that these enemies of your future leave your table – that they are not invited guests and have no authority to stay.

Replacing lies with truth

False statement: I am unlovable and unworthy. If you knew the real me, you would reject me. No one really likes me.

Truth statement: With God's help, I will learn to be myself and trust Him to bring people into my life that will appreciate me and respect me for who I am. My worth is in who God says I am.

'But the very hairs on your head are numbered. Do not

75

fear therefore; you are of more value than many sparrows.' Luke 12:7

'God made him who had no sin (Jesus) to be sin for us, so that in him we might become the righteousness of God.' 2 Corinthians 5:21

'To the praise of his glorious grace, which he has freely given us in the One he loves. In him we have redemption through his blood, the forgiveness of sins, in accordance with the riches of God's grace.' Ephesians 1:6-7

False statement: Even when I do my best, it is not good enough. I can never meet the standard.

Truth statement: I am fully loved, completely accepted and totally pleasing to God. Regardless of how much I do or fail to do, I will remain fully loved, completely accepted, and totally pleasing to God. I choose to surrender to Him, finding my faith in Him and trusting His ability to sustain me. I will seek to be a God-pleaser, not a people-pleaser.

'If the Lord delights in a man's way, he makes his steps firm; although he stumble, he will not fall, for the Lord upholds him with his hand.' Psalm 37:23-24.

'I can do all things through Christ who strengthens me.' Philippians 4:13

'But seek first his kingdom and his righteousness, and all these things will be given to you as well.' Matthew 6:33

False statement: I will always be insecure and fearful. I am a bad person.

Truth statement: I can be confident in Him who created me. I will draw my security, courage, and identity from what God says about me.

> 'For God did not give us a spirit of timidity, but a spirit of power, of love and of self-discipline.' 2 Timothy 1:7

> 'You, dear children, are from God and have overcome them, because the one who is in you is greater than the one who is in the world.' 1 John 4:4

> 'There is no fear in love. But perfect love drives out fear, because fear has to do with punishment. The one who fears is not made perfect in love.' 1 John 4:18

> 'Be strong and courageous. Do not be terrified; do not be discouraged, for the Lord your God is with you wherever you go.' Joshua 1:8-9

False Statement: I always make wrong decisions. I am unable to take care of myself or make wise decisions. I am out there all alone.

Truth Statement: I choose to believe that God will help me to make wise decisions as I ask Him for direction for my life. If I align my decisions with the word of God, I will consistently make the right choice. God will protect me and keep me.

> 'If any of you lacks wisdom, he should ask God, who gives generously to all without finding fault, and it will be given to him.' James 1:5

'Call to me and I will answer you and tell you great and unsearchable things you do not know.' Jeremiah 33:3
'Your word is a lamp for my feet and a light for my path.' Psalm 119:105

'Trust in the Lord with all your heart and lean not on your own understanding; in all your ways acknowledge him, and he will make your paths straight.' Psalm 3:5-6

'If you remain in me and my words remain in you, ask whatever you wish, and it will be given you.' John 15:7

False Statement: I will always be lonely.

Truth Statement: God says He sets the solitary in families. I choose to believe that He will see to it that I will always belong to a family and have friends, if I show myself to be friendly.

'God sets the lonely in families, he leads forth the prisoners with singing; but the rebellious live in a sun-scorched land.' Psalm 68:6

'A man who has friends must himself be friendly, but there is a friend who sticks closer than a brother.' Psalm 18:24

'Delight yourself in the Lord and He will give you the desires of your heart. Commit your way to the Lord; trust in him and he will do this.' Psalm 37:4-5

These are just a few examples of ways to capture your thoughts and make them obedient to the truth of Jesus.

Doing this is not a crisis response; not a nacre response that you pull out for whenever life gets tough.

This is part of the everyday normal Christian walk, a nacre response that not only deals with intruders but recognises that thoughts are like weeds; they will stifle the true vine if left unchecked. In order to produce a pearl amidst pain, to triumph in trouble, we must be those who learn to wield the sword of His Word to divide truth and lies and then do what no other being in creation can do for us, not even God – we choose to believe.

From Pain to Pearls

Chapter 8: Broken Praise

I heard a story once about a baby girl who contracted meningitis and was rushed to hospital by her parents. They feared the worst as the doctors told them she was at death's door. Along with their church family, the parents prayed, fasted and cried out to God for her healing and when daylight came, she had not only lived through the night but was totally healed without any sign of meningitis left in her body.

As the parents drove their daughter home, the car filled with the sound of their worship, and they praised and thanked God for her miraculous recovery. It was at that moment that God spoke to the father and asked him a question that has made a deep impression on me ever since I heard this tale.

He asked: 'Would you still be praising me if she'd died?'

> **Bringing Him our praises, our heartfelt worship and adoration is a powerful nacre response to pain and adversity.**

It's a deep question, with deep implications. It asks us about our motive for worship, our motive for bringing Him our praises. Are we those who bring praise and thanksgiving only when life is good or have we come to understand that God is good all the time, even when the circumstances of our lives lead us to believe otherwise?

Bringing Him our praises, our heartfelt worship and adoration is a powerful nacre response to pain and adversity and is found throughout the scriptures. I think there's a reason why the Bible refers to us bringing a *sacrifice* of praise. It's because the times when we least feel like thanksgiving and worship, yet lift our voice anyway, are the most powerful. Those are the times when praising Him feels like a sacrifice, when worshipping Him costs us.

> Psalm 54:6 'I will sacrifice a freewill offering to you; I will praise your name, Lord, for it is good.'
>
> Jonah 2:9 'But I, with shouts of grateful praise, will sacrifice to you. What I have vowed I will make good. I will say, "Salvation comes from the Lord."'
>
> Hebrews 13:15 'Through Jesus, therefore, let us continually offer to God a sacrifice of praise – the fruit of lips that openly profess his name.'

These scriptures are really clear. Worship is a free-will offering given to our Lord because He is good. We worship because salvation comes from Him and as we open our lips and openly profess His name, He 'inhabits' our praises (Psalm 22:2-4). This means that when we praise Him, we provide a means whereby He can draw close to us; a space for Him to live.

It says in Psalm 100:4 that we enter His gates with thanksgiving; that there is a password into His presence and that word is 'thank you'.

Gratitude is a powerful force in the face of adversity, mainly because it ushers us into the presence of our gracious God. There is something about gratitude that elicits a grace response from our Father. As a parent myself I know how it feels when my children are grateful for the things they have- gratitude speaks of beauty and goodness in their hearts and it invites me to continue to give to them.

In Luke 17:19 (King James version) we see Jesus' response to gratitude when one of ten lepers who were all 'made clean' comes back to thank Jesus and brings glory to God. Jesus tells this one, this man who chose to come back and glorify God with thanks and worship that he is now 'made whole'.

When we choose to respond with the nacre of gratitude during our times of trial and adversity, I believe we elicit from the heart of God a deeper level of healing and restoration, not because God has favourites but because gratitude and worship causes us to interact with God for longer and in His presence there are treasures to be found.

Ten lepers went on their way, nine of them may never have spoken to Jesus again, never had the opportunity to interact with Him again- but one came back. His choice to place himself before Jesus with nothing but praise on His lips created an opportunity for God to show His favour and grace once again in this man's life.

Now, I'm not suggesting that we should be thankful *for* the abuse or sickness or loss: how can we be thankful to Him for something that hasn't come from Him? I am suggesting that we are thankful *in* it. We can recognise that the trouble we are facing is not good, not perfect and not uplifting, but through our gratitude to a perfect, good and uplifting God, we enter into a divine exchange. Our trouble for His triumph, our ashes for His beauty, our weakness for His strength. More often than not, this divine exchange has happened in my life when I have chosen to worship Him, despite my emotions.

When I have lingered in His presence for longer than necessary, before Him on my knees in an attitude of thankfulness and praise, I have found not only cleansing, but wholeness.

Through the magnifying glass

Circumstances can have a way of making themselves look really big and making us feel very small. Some circumstances we face can even make God seem small. When we find ourselves facing more than we can handle on our own and when our trouble presses down on us, we have to make a free-will offering, a choice to open up our mouths and magnify His name above every other name.

As we magnify Him, as we make Him bigger, the things we are facing do not necessarily change but they certainly shrink in ferocity within our minds. Our perception of who we are and who He is in the situation changes when we magnify Him.

I remember a few years ago finding myself in a situation that made me feel so small. I was facing a giant and it looked as if it was going to tear down everything I had spent years building up. Slander and gossip surrounded me and as I stood in my kitchen preparing lunch, all I could think about was this giant I faced. It was like wave after wave of despair came crashing over me, and I felt as if I might drown under the weight of it. Panic began to rise, my heart rate went up and even in the safety of my own kitchen, I felt completely exposed.

During those few moments of hopelessness and despair, I heard the whisper of the Holy Spirit as He urged me: 'Right now,' He said, 'choose joy.'

And even though I had no idea how to choose an emotion I did not feel, I decided to be obedient. Just at that moment, a really old worship song began to form on my lips ... and I whispered it to myself:

> 'Rejoice in the Lord always, again I say rejoice; rejoice in the Lord always, again I say rejoice. Rejoice, rejoice; again I say rejoice. Rejoice, rejoice; again I say rejoice.'

It started as a whisper but as I sang it again and again, I commanded my internal emotions to line up with the words I was declaring, and before I knew it, I was shouting the song at the top of my voice, marching up and down my kitchen and waving my butter-knife in the air. It was at this point that my husband came into the room, took one look at me and my knife and walked straight back out again. We've been married long enough for him to know when he just needs to leave me to it!

The situation I faced did not change in that moment, but the giant I faced did. The giant wasn't the situation; the giant was what I had created in my mind, the emotions that ruled my thoughts and made me feel as if I was drowning.

Singing that song of worship and praise focused my mind on things above; it changed my perspective and I declared that my joy was in God, not in my circumstances. Worshipping Him despite how I felt released a nacre response that enabled me to receive His grace and ride out the storm. My emotions were obedient to my lips and as I sang, joy filled my heart; the kind of joy that comes from being right with God, not right with circumstances. I found the strength I needed to carry on.

Paul puts it like this in 2 Corinthians 12:9 when he shares with us what God told him in response to his cry for help.

> 'My grace is enough; it's all you need. My strength comes into its own in your weakness.' (The Message)

When we choose to focus on Him through worship, praise and thanksgiving, we allow God to make nacre for us!

Paul goes on to tell us:

> 'Once I heard that, I was glad to let it happen. I quit focusing on the handicap and began appreciating the gift. It was a case of Christ's strength moving in on my weakness. Now I take limitations in stride, and with good cheer, these limitations that cut me down to size—abuse, accidents, opposition, bad breaks. I just let Christ take over! And so the weaker I get, the stronger I become.'

When we choose to focus on Him through worship, praise and thanksgiving, we allow God to make nacre for us! Grace enables us to have a godly response to the troubles we face; worshipping Him amidst our adversity is how we let Him take over. James 1 puts it like this:

² 'Dear brothers and sisters, when troubles come your way, consider it an opportunity for great joy. For you know that when your faith is tested, your endurance has a chance to grow. So let it grow, for when your endurance is fully developed, you will be perfect and complete, needing nothing.'

Praising in your prison

Acts 16:22-29 tells the story of Paul and Silas who were beaten, flogged and then thrown into jail. I don't know about you but that would have a serious impact on my desire to worship; especially when the reason I'm going through the pain is because of my service to God!

But as the story unfolds, it becomes clear that their nacre response of worship, praise and prayer released a response from heaven that ultimately broke down their prison doors and set not only them free but all those around them too.

The pain we go through, the emotions that come with that pain and the untenable situations we sometimes face can make us feel trapped inside a prison. We can be in captivity when we've done nothing other than serve God to get us there. We did everything right, and yet we still find that life can beat us, flog us and throw us into a prison of despair and depression.

We can become so overwhelmed by disappointment in God and the feeling that He should've taken care of us better – that this is not how life was supposed to turn out – that it steals any desire we may have to worship Him. Why would we worship what can appear to be the very source of the trouble we find ourselves in?

But the truth is that God is good, and that His face is turned towards us, though we are not promised a pain-free life. The truth is that we have an enemy who comes to kill, steal and destroy. The truth is that we are the victims of other people's bad choices and the victims of our own bad choices.

Sometimes there is no reason other than the sad truth that bad things do happen to good people. When we come to terms with the fact that we've been beaten, flogged and thrown into jail, when we've admitted our fear and our anger, when all is said and done, we are left with a choice of how to respond.

> **How we respond to pain and adversity is always a stronger testimony than anything we may do when life is treating us kindly.**

How we respond to pain and adversity is always a stronger testimony than anything we may do when life is treating us kindly. The community around us does not need us to show them a perfectly neat and presentable life, without a hint of challenge or trouble about it. The world needs to see the strength of believers who despite their pain and trouble choose to lift their voice in prayer and praise and see their deliverance come.

Living in the 'but'

There are those who believe that Lucifer (Satan) was heaven's worship leader. There are passages to suggest that he at least had access to musical instruments and that he was high above the other angels; an Archangel along with Michael and Gabriel (See Ezekiel 28 and Isaiah 14). I'm not a theologian, so I won't declare this to be undeniable truth, but it does stand to reason that Satan would have a particular hatred for worship of the Most High, as the Bible tells us clearly and without ambiguity what the condition of Satan's heart was like:

> Isaiah 14: 'How you are fallen from heaven, O Lucifer, son of the morning...For you have said in your heart: "I will ascend into heaven, I will exalt my throne above the stars of God; I will also sit on the mount of the congregation on the farthest sides of the north; I will ascend above the heights of the clouds, I will be like the Most High."'

This context helps me understand why so often when we face difficulties, trials or adversities, the last thing we want to do is worship. The enemy has a vested interest in keeping us separated from God's presence: he comes to kill, steal and destroy and prowls around like a lion seeking those whom he may devour (John 10:10).

He wants to steal our peace, kill our hope and destroy our relationship with God and each other. Paul warns us not to be unaware of the enemy's schemes (2 Corinthians 2:11) and so we need to know that worshipping God when we least feel like it is a key nacre response to adversity.

When we worship God with all our hearts, despite the struggles we are having, we fly in the face of all the harm the enemy has planned for us and we frustrate him by constantly taking our problems into the presence of our King. I imagine there's nowhere the enemy wants to be less than in the presence of God, so when we open our mouths and sing praises to the

From Pain to Pearls

Most High, when we invite the presence of God to fill our hearts, our homes and our lives, we make it very uncomfortable for the enemy to stay around.

There is a great example of this in the story of Queen Esther. Esther had been told of Haman's plot to annihilate her people and after showing great courage, she had found favour with the King. Her response to the threat from Haman was to bring him into the King's presence. She laid a banquet in the presence of her enemy and there found that her enemy's power was completely usurped by that of her King. (Esther 7)

When we worship despite our feelings, despite our pain and suffering, we do the same thing. We bring those feelings into the King's presence and by His grace and favour we are able to discover that in His presence there is fullness of joy (Psalm 16:11) a joy that can find a way to hope and life where there seemed no way.

King David did this too. He understood something about the power of worship. In Psalm 42:5 David asks himself why he feels so down. He questions his own emotional state and then makes a decision to command his emotions to worship the Lord. It reminds me of what happened in my kitchen when I sang His praises.

It was like a life belt of hope and joy and strength was thrust into my hands amidst a storm, simply by choosing to take responsibility for my own emotions and command myself to worship, despite them.

In fact throughout the Psalms, David constantly faces impossible situations. He comes up against hostility, opposition and grief and each time it looks as if he's about to

90

throw in the towel until he says: 'But...' He turns his attention away from himself, away from the trouble and fixes his eyes on heaven. King David learnt how to live in the 'but'.

Take a look at these examples:

Psalm 73:26
'My flesh and my heart may fail, *but* God is the strength of my heart and my portion forever.'

Psalm 74:9 & 12
'We are given no signs from God; no prophets are left, and none of us knows how long this will be. *But* God is my King from long ago; he brings salvation on the earth.'

Psalm 69:7-13
'For I endure scorn for your sake, and shame covers my face. I am a foreigner to my own family, a stranger to my own mother's children; Those who sit at the gate mock me, and I am the song of the drunkards. *But* I pray to you, Lord, in the time of your favour; in your great love, O God, answer me with your sure salvation.'

Psalm 118:10-14
'All the nations surrounded me, *but* in the name of the Lord I cut them down. They surrounded me on every side, *but* in the name of the Lord I cut them down. They swarmed around me like bees, *but* in the name of the Lord I cut them down. I was pushed back and about to fall, *but* the Lord helped me. The Lord is my strength and my defence; he has become my salvation.'

Jesus is our salvation. He is our hope, He is our joy, He is our strength, He is our rock, He is our anchor, He is our source, He is our peace, He is our all-in-all.

He is worthy of all praise and all worship; all honour and glory is His and as His people, our responsibility is to remind ourselves of who we are in Christ, and who He is in us. Do not let the troubles of this life tear you down and rip you away from the reason you were created: to bring glory to His Name.

No matter what you are facing today, whether you have suffered tremendous loss, or heartache or pain; whether you fear for your future or fear for your past; whether you struggle to believe that you will ever feel joy again or be able to dream again; I want to encourage you to live in the 'but'.

Understand that what you can see with your human eyes is not the full story.

Understand that what you can see with your human eyes is not the full story; there is another chapter. There is the part where you open up your mouth, where you silence the voice of doubt, of fear and disappointment and you ask yourself: 'Why are you so downcast oh my soul, why so dismayed within me … I will yet praise the Lord!'

Realise today that broken worship and painful praise is nacre; it's a life-saving response to pain and adversity and not only will it protect you from the corroding influence of pressure and stress, it will produce inside of you a pearl of such value that God Himself will harvest it.

From Pain to Pearls

Chapter 9:

With A Friend You Can Face The Worst

It is at this point that our oyster and its nacre responses to adversity loses its similarity to that of us humans; here the analogy ends. Oysters go it alone; there is no sense of community or mutual support to be had during times of trouble if you're an oyster. You release your nacre or you don't, either way it's only your own life that's at stake and none will mourn your loss- such is the harsh reality of the oyster's existence.

But for us people things are different, or at least they should be. We were never meant to go it alone. It is in our very DNA to belong, to be connected to others and to want to do life in partnership with people. Sadly for many of us, life is made more difficult by a deep sense of loneliness and isolation, especially during times of difficulty.

This is what Ecclesiastes 4:9-12 has to say about it:

> 'It's better to have a partner than go it alone. Share the work, share the wealth. And if one falls down, the other helps. But if there's no one to help, tough! Two in a bed warm each other. Alone, you shiver all night. By yourself you're unprotected. With a friend you can face the worst. Can you round up a third? A three-stranded rope isn't easily snapped.' (The Message)

This scripture is clear: one of our nacre responses to adversity, to pain and trouble includes sharing our burden with a friend.

'With a friend you can face the worst' is my favourite verse in that passage — what a statement! With a friend by your side your burden is halved, your protection is doubled and you are not easily snapped.

No wonder the enemy seeks to separate us out from each other, no wonder he wants to see us suffer in silence, alone and unsupported! In the same way that a lion on the hunt will separate its prey from the herd, so the lion that seeks to kill, steal and destroy us will employ the same tactics.

There is a nacre response available to us called transparency: a humble call for help from those around us that will strengthen our ability to turn whatever pain we are facing into pearls.

The trouble is that most of us don't like to ask for help. We don't like to communicate need. There's something about showing weakness that makes us feel uncomfortable. We don't want to appear vulnerable or unable to cope with the demands of life. And so we pretend.

There is a difference between fact and truth.

Behind the façade

We pretend that our marriages are perfect, we pretend that our kids are loving God, we pretend that we are always healthy, we pretend that we are always happy; surely anything less falls below the expected standard of our Christianity?

Being a faith-filled Christian does not mean you deny the facts of the circumstances of your life.

There is a difference between fact and truth. For instance, not telling anyone that you've lost your job does not change the fact; what it does is cover you in shame and isolate you from those who could be standing in faith with you and believing with you to see your circumstance change.

Pretending that your marriage isn't struggling only creates a false reality that prevents you from reaching out for wisdom from those who've been there before. Pretending that you are healthy when in fact you have symptoms that should be checked by a doctor only prevents you from receiving professional help your life may later depend on.

Is there maybe a perception amongst us as God's people that living a life without difficulty or trouble is a sign of God's approval or special blessing? True, when we live planted in His Word and we are operating in the principles of the Kingdom of God, then I believe we attract the blessing of God, but that does not mean our lives are always trouble free: we already established that in earlier chapters. Yet many of us fear people's judgement, the same whispers that haunted Job: 'what did you do to deserve this disaster, how did you displease God?'

This mind-set can cause us to become those who erect a façade, like the old movie sets in Hollywood. Everything looks just as it should on the outside but step behind the scenes and you'll see the ugly scaffolding holding it all together. So we make sure no one gets to see behind the scenes.

This response to adversity is not a nacre response: to hide all our trouble under the carpet of 'Christian happiness' is based on shame, fear and control and it dates right back to the first instance this earth ever had of pain and trouble; Adam and Eve in the garden of Eden.

In Genesis 3:8-10 we see the construction of Adam and Eve's façade by the sewing together of fig leaves to hide their shame.

> 'At that moment their eyes were opened, and they suddenly felt shame at their nakedness. So they sewed fig leaves together to cover themselves. When the cool evening breezes were blowing, the man and his wife heard the Lord God walking about in the garden. So they hid from the Lord God among the trees. Then the Lord God called to the man, "Where are you?" He replied, "I heard you walking in the garden, so I hid. I was afraid because I was naked."'

Another way to interpret it is this: 'I am in trouble, I am facing a difficult situation and now I don't know what to do with this sense of vulnerability, so I will hide my shame and exercise control over what part of me and my life you get to see.'

Imagine driving to a friend's house and getting lost along the way. You have no map, no satnav and so you call and ask for directions. The first question your friend will ask you is: 'Where are you?' Much like God asked of Adam and Eve.

Now imagine being so ashamed of how lost you actually are that you can't bear to tell your friend the extent of your situation. You might pretend that you are closer than you really are.

Perhaps you'd say you were 10 miles closer to the destination to cover over your embarrassment. Whilst this course of action might help you feel a bit better about yourself, the directions your friend would give you would be useless. They would not make sense, nor would they help you get to where you are going.

When we are lost, we need to ask for help and when we ask for help, we need to be real about our starting point.

The fact of the matter is, when we are lost, we need to ask for help and when we ask for help, we need to be real about our starting point. The same is true when we are faced with life's difficulties. We need to commit to being transparent with those we trust, open about our progress and real about our struggles.

Entering into a cycle of shame, fear and control will disable our ability to draw on others for strength, for comfort, for wisdom and for support. It will undermine the very purposes of partnership, both with God and with people. When times are hard and we are struggling to believe God's Word, we need a friend to believe with us.

When we doubt our ability to pray any longer, we need a friend to pray on our behalf; when we can't lift our hands in worship, we need a friend to lift them for us.

In the words of Samwise Gamgee, Frodo's faithful friend in the *Lord of the Rings* trilogy: 'I may not be able to carry the ring, but I can carry you.'

True grit

Being open and honest with those close to us about what we are facing is powerful beyond measure.

This nacre of transparency is in itself a powerful response to pain and adversity. We were born to do life in partnership with God and with people. When God created humanity in the form of one man, He said: 'It is not good for man to be alone' (Genesis 2:18). And so He created another human being.

Whilst ever we live our lives behind a façade, created to present ourselves to those around us in a more favourable light, we will limit our ability to have real connections with people and what's more, we will cease to have a real impact on a world that is crying out for authenticity.

___

Real pearls are valued because of the process they have been through.

Pearls are valuable because of the process they have been through in order to become what they are. You can go to a market stall and buy perfect pearls, shaped to perfection, shiny and smooth but they are practically worthless. Those plastic pearls are mass produced: a cheap counterfeit of a process that is nothing less than miraculous.

The real pearls, the ones we place the highest value on are rare. They are naturally produced and their authenticity is measured by the irregular shape and the grit that can be seen within the very fabric of the nacre. Real pearls are imperfect, real pearls have grit. Real pearls are valued because of the process they have been through.

To me, Queen Esther's story is a perfect example of the need for transparency as part of our nacre response to adversity and trouble. Let me show you how her courage to be real – to be authentic – produced a pearl that not only saved her own life, but that of a nation.

From reject to royalty

A childhood spent in Sunday school led me to believe that the story of Esther was the Bible's version of a fairytale. She seemed like a Disney princess to me: dressed in fine clothes and after spending 12 months in a beauty spa, she was chosen by the prince as the fairest of them all. Surely it was a fairytale with singing animals and a fairy Godmother being the only things missing.

I never learned in Sunday school that Esther was a refugee child of perhaps 12-16 years old. I never knew that she was not given a choice in the matter; a vulnerable young orphaned girl, taken from her home by soldiers. I never understood that she would have been groomed by her 'teachers' to bring sexual pleasure to a man she feared, or that she might only ever see him once and then spend the rest of her life among the other women considered the King's sexual property.

Realising that Esther was more akin to a trafficked victim than a Disney princess makes me sit up and take notice; it makes me

101

view her with a new-found respect that has made me read
between the lines of this well-known tale and see what I didn
makes me n
Esther's story is a message of hope, of purpose and of destiny
for every one of us. There are universal principles and lessons
at work in this story that apply to each of us and if we learn
from her we too can become what she became: a voice for the
voiceless, a defender of the weak, an ambassador for the
Kingdom of God.

Even the fact that God is never mentioned throughout the
story gives me comfort, as I can pinpoint seasons in my life
where I've felt far away and removed from Him and yet in
hindsight I can see His hand was all over the situation.

Esther went from reject to royalty and so can we. We can be
those who don't let our past determine our future. Whatever
our external circumstances, background or situations may be
like, we can decide to respond to bad things from a good place
and create pearls from our pain.

Esther was marked out from the crowd, not because of her
external beauty – she was in a crowd of the most beautiful
women of her time – she was marked out because of her
internal beauty. Our character and how we carry ourselves
shines through, whatever our exterior may be. Our life
experiences can turn us into victims, wracked with bitterness,
anger and unforgiveness, or we can allow Jesus to turn our pain
into pearls of great value.

In Esther 4 we read how the King had made a decree that
would wipe out the Jews. Mordecai, Esther's uncle, who had
originally told Esther to hide her true identity as a Jew and an
orphan, now implores Esther to drop her façade, to speak up
and reveal her true identity:

13 And Mordecai told them to answer Esther: "Do not think in your heart that you will escape in the king's palace any more than all the other Jews. 14 For if you remain completely silent at this time, relief and deliverance will arise for the Jews from another place, but you and your father's house will perish. Yet who knows whether you have come to the kingdom for *such* a time as this?"

It is estimated that Esther had at this point been Queen for around 5 years. Her façade was well established and had kept her safe, away from prying eyes and awkward questions about her past. She had power and influence and her uncle's request to open up her shell as it were and reveal the pearl she had produced was a frightening prospect.

So often when we have worked hard behind the scenes to build up our scaffolding, to keep the façade upright, the thought of opening up to people about what our story contains is frightening. But I believe, as in Esther's story, that many lives and many breakthroughs can be found on the other side of our courage to speak out.

There is always a season when we are right in the middle of releasing nacre, when we are fighting to stay alive on the inside where that façade is needed- it becomes the shell that hides the pearl until it is fully formed. However, I am convinced that those pearls of great value are never meant to stay within the shell. Our stories are not meant to stay inside of us.

Revelation 12:11 says it like this:

> They overcame him by the blood of the Lamb and by
> the word of their testimony; they did not love their lives
> so much as to shrink from death.

You see, the world is looking for authenticity not perfection. So
often we think that we need to impress people with our great
lives, our nice ducks all in a row and we don't realise that
everyone is just looking for authenticity. Where are the real
people dealing with real issues in a real way? That's what the
world is asking. Who can help us find a way through this
difficult terrain? Not the people who present perfection,
unattainable and clearly fake. But those whose lives are full of
grit, imperfect in their shape but invaluable in the lessons learnt
along the way.

That's the witness, that's how we overcome the enemy. By the
blood of the Lamb and the power of our testimony. Not 'we
are Christian therefore we never have any problems', no, 'we
are human therefore we have the same challenges as you but we
have a God who grows us, molds us, shapes us and helps us
overcome whatever life may throw our way'. That's being real
and that is very, very powerful.

Esther could have been an ornament and lived a life of comfort
in her royal position but she came to understand that she was
born for purpose, just like we all are. We cannot become
people who simply take all the benefits of Christianity- the
favour, the redemption, forgiveness, wholeness and restoration
without any of the responsibility. We cannot become those
who release nacre and produce a pearl of great value, simply to
hide it away inside a dark shell.

> Those of us who are strong and able in the faith need
> to step in and lend a hand to those who falter, and not
> just do what is most convenient for us. Strength is for

service not status. Each one of us needs to look after the good of the people around us, asking ourselves: How can I help? (Romans 15 - The Message)

Strength is for service not status and instead of simply enjoying the influence and position of royalty that we have attained through Him, we can become a voice. We can become vessels, ambassadors for freedom instead of simply ornaments in the house of the King.

Our lives are not fairytales, they do not have magic wands and princes that wake us with a kiss but we do have a Saviour. We have a God that takes our broken, vulnerable selves and calls us to be agents of change. He says to each of us- young, old, male, female, rich or poor the same thing spoken to Esther - we were born for such a time as this.

From Pain to Pearls

Chapter 10: Purpose In The Pain

It was March 2005 when we got the keys to what would become the first Mercy Ministries UK home. My parents were visiting and I had decided to show them around the property, hoping they would be inspired by the beauty of the place. The sexual abuse my sister Debbie had suffered had hit my parents hard – how could they not have seen or known about it and why had God not intervened?

They had served Him, laid their lives down for His Kingdom and yet they had suffered this tragedy, and many more besides. He could have told them, or shown them or in some way prevented this terrible thing happening but He didn't … and so they were left with broken pieces of their faith and an overwhelming sense of sadness and disappointment.

Debbie had graduated from Mercy Ministries of America four years prior to this day and she was doing well, but my mother in particular was still struggling to make sense of her own pain. Walking around the grounds we began to talk about the many broken young women Mercy UK would reach: the lives transformed and hope restored.

As we chatted, my mother began to cry. With tears in her eyes she looked at my sister and I and said: 'It's been a long time since I've heard God speak to me, but I just heard Him tell me that there was purpose in the pain.'

She took our hands and with that steely determination she is known and loved for, she said: 'Every girl that graduates from this place will be a little piece of my healing.'

My mother came to one of the first graduations we ever had at Mercy UK and in the wonderful way that only God can do, the very first girl who graduated from the UK programme was Scottish: and for my very patriotic Scottish mother, that was a kiss from heaven...

Romans 8:28 tells us that God works all things together for the good of those who love the Lord and are called according to His purpose.

All things: that means both good things and bad things. He works all things together. This doesn't mean that He sends all things to us; we already addressed the fact that God cannot give what He does not have, but it does mean that whatever we face, it is not too big or too painful for Him not to be found in the midst of it.

God is in it with you

In Daniel 3, we read the story of Shadrach, Meshach and Abednego; servants of God who defied the King and refused to bow down to him. Their refusal to be disobedient to God and buckle under the pressure of their circumstance put them in harm's way. Their response to this situation is profound; in verses 16-18 they say:

> 'King Nebuchadnezzar, we do not need to defend ourselves before you in this matter. If we are thrown into the blazing furnace, the God we serve is able to deliver us from it, and he will deliver us from Your Majesty's hand. But even if he does not, we want you to know, Your Majesty, that we will not serve your gods or worship the image of gold you have set up.'

What follows is a famous miracle and has been retold by every Sunday school teacher since. They were thrown into a fire so hot that the soldiers who carried them there were burned alive, and yet when the king looked into the furnace, he saw not three men but four.

Verse 26 carries on the tale:

> 'So Shadrach, Meshach and Abednego came out of the fire, and the satraps, prefects, governors and royal advisors crowded around them. They saw that the fire had not harmed their bodies, nor was a hair on their heads singed; their robes were not scorched, and there was no smell of fire on them.'

I have seen over the years many who have been through such tremendous pain that it should have burned them up as in a furnace. The loss of a child, the break-up of a marriage, the body riddled with disease or innocence stolen by an abuser, and yet through the unconditional love of God, the power of forgiveness and the life-transforming truths found in the Word, they have walked away from that furnace of devastation, alive and with hope for their future. Many of them don't even smell of fire; there is no hint on them that they have faced what they've faced and when you hear them speak of it, their healing is so complete that it increases your own level of hope and belief in a God who can perform the miraculous.

This is what happened to King Nebuchadnezzar when he saw the miracle of redemption (verses 28-29):

> 'Then Nebuchadnezzar said, 'Praise be to the God of Shadrach, Meshach and Abednego, who has sent his angel and rescued his servants! They trusted in him and

defied the king's command and were willing to give up their lives rather than serve or worship any god except their own God. Therefore I decree that the people of any nation or language who say anything against the God of Shadrach, Meshach and Abednego be cut into pieces and their houses be turned into piles of rubble, for no other god can save in this way.'

What the king meant for evil God turned around, simply by His presence in the situation.' He was with them in the fire and His presence was of such significance that the whole nation turned to God.

What situation are you facing today that represents this furnace? Do you feel the heat of it, do you fear the damage it could cause you? Be encouraged today that God is in this with you: His Name is Emmanuel, 'God with us.' He is not watching from afar, assessing your ability to respond to this pain and judging you on your performance.

Don't confuse struggle with failure. They are not the same thing.

Don't confuse struggle with failure. They are not the same thing. God has no vested interest in our failure. His desire is to see us succeed and to grow.

If you are struggling, reach into Him. Scripture tells us that He is close to the broken hearted (Psalm 34:18) and that as we draw near to Him, He will draw near to us. (James 4:8). If you want God to get you out of trouble, then invite him into it.

Skyfall

Drawing near to Him is vital during times of trial and adversity. Yet somehow we humans have an 'I'll do it on my own, in my own way' default setting when it comes to navigating challenges. For some reason God can begin to feel very far away from us and our trouble and before we know it, that sense of 'God with us' has disappeared.

When it was my 40th birthday, I decided it was best celebrated by doing something crazy, like a skydive. At 15,000 ft high, with a 60 second free-fall of 130 mph it was, I calculated, just enough adrenaline to stop me feeling old.

I had opted for the tandem skydive: the one where the risks are reduced by the fact that you are strapped to a highly trained professional! I arrived at the skydive centre and waited for the fear to set in, but it never came. It turned out that overcoming fear wasn't going to be my lesson that day, it was something else entirely.

You see, I have been married for 21 years and the only man I allow into my personal space is my husband. It hadn't occurred to me (for some unknown reason) that being strapped to a highly trained professional meant that I would have a complete stranger tied to me. It wasn't until the man introduced himself to me and showed me the harness we would share that I began to feel the butterflies of the awkward discomfort of close proximity.

However, during the training, the instructor said something that changed everything for me. He said: 'I do this all day every day. If you stay close to me, work with me and not against me and do exactly what I tell you to do, I will land you safely on the ground.'

It was in that moment that God showed me what the lesson was going to be. Why do so many of us insist on jumping out of the aeroplane of our lives alone and unaccompanied? Why do we put ourselves through the rigmarole of trying to remember the dos and don'ts, counting down the seconds until we hit the ground, hoping we do everything we are supposed to do to avoid serious injury or worse, death?

God is an expert at living life: He wrote the manual!

God is an expert at living life: He wrote the manual! He will make sure we land safely, despite the obvious dangers. When we hit free-fall in life – when the speed seems out of control and we can't remember what we are supposed to do – then isn't it worth pushing past our own personal discomfort to embrace intimacy with a God who has promised to land us safely?

There is such power in relinquishing our need to pull all the strings and in trusting Him enough to listen to what He says; to work with Him and not against Him. He is Emmanuel, God with us. But He is a gentleman and waits both for our permission and our compliance before He steps into our personal space.

I will never forget those 60 seconds; that leap out of a plane into the clouds below. It took the breath out of my lungs, shook my body with the force of a tornado and sent my mind completely blank. My initial awkwardness forgotten, I was so grateful for the man strapped close behind me whose strength I borrowed, who directed me with calm instruction and whose perspective showed me that we can see this either as falling or flying!

In the same way, when we feel we are in free-fall in our lives, we can reach to Him for the strength we don't have, the patience we've run out of and the wisdom we've forgotten. He is willing and able to lend you His strength, increase your patience and remind you of the things you already know. In fact, according to Jeremiah 33:3 when we call upon Him, He'll even tell us deep and unsearchable things that we do not know: what an invitation!

Formed in the deep

My friend sat across from me, smiling her beautiful smile. It had been a long time since I'd seen her smile like that, as most of the previous year had stripped her of everything she held dear. Her heart had been broken by the man she loved for 17 years and today was the day that the divorce had come through. She sipped her drink and as she looked at me, I asked her how she was feeling now that there was a line drawn in the sand.

'I'm surprisingly ok,' she said 'mainly because God showed me this incredible vision the other day and it has saved me from drowning during the stormy shipwreck my life has become.'

I asked her what picture God had shown her and so she told me about a vision she had seen of herself being in a shipwreck. The storm was raging and as the waves crashed over the edge, the ship of her life gave way and she was thrown overboard. Desperately she clung on to the pieces she could see floating around her – her sense of value, identity, hopes and dreams – pieces of her life that seemed to float just out of reach.

The weight of everything that was on her and what she was trying to keep hold of was pulling her under and the debris of her shipwrecked life was flying around in the wind, threatening her safety. She was weary of the fight and tired of trying to keep her head above the stormy water.

Kicking with all her might, she managed to break the surface of the waves and catch her breath every now and again. A nagging fear in the back of her mind wondered how long she could do this for until she would simply drown in the midst of what was left of her previously perfect life. And then she cried out to God. She thought He would throw her a life-line, or miraculously calm the storm, but instead He told her to dive down into the deep.

Psalm 42:7-8 describes it like this:

> 'Deep calls to deep in the roar of the water; all the waves and breakers have swept over me. By day the Lord directs his love, at night his song is with me – a prayer to the God of my life.'

And as my friend chose to dive under and swim into the depths of God, she became aware of a calmness under the sea of her relentless circumstances. The storm raged high above but under the ocean there was safety and stillness. And here's the miracle: the storm didn't stop. The debris was still flying around on the surface, but instead of trying to breathe by risking her life on top of the water, she dived down under and into God and found that she could breathe underwater. He supernaturally gave her an ability to do the impossible: to stay

114

alive in a circumstance that would otherwise be the emotional and spiritual death of her.

In reality, God was teaching her that His ways are higher than our ways, that even when we think we are going to drown, if we throw ourselves into the depths of His love and compassion, if we choose to respond with the nacre responses described in this book, He will breathe for us.

Revelation is not transformation. If you say you know and don't do – you don't know!

'Diving down deep' means choosing to be obedient to His word. It means releasing the nacre of forgiveness, the nacre of a renewed mind. It means worshipping Him for who He is, not for how good our life is; it means praying, giving, and operating with gratitude. All of these nacre responses are ways of diving into the deep of the things of God and finding that when we do, we can breathe underwater.

Treasures out of darkness

It's in the depths of the ocean, in the darkness under the sea, that the creation of pearls takes place. And the same goes for us; it's during the storms of life and the darkness of our circumstances that we come across a life or death choice. We get to choose our response.

Will we let this pain or hurt or disappointment take us out? Will we let the violation we have suffered be the end of us, or will we engage in the process designed by God to keep us intact? Will our lives and all that we have experienced steal away our hope, our sense of self and leave us with nothing but an empty shell or will we release those nacre responses and produce a pearl that not only saves our lives but brings glory to our Maker?

There is no one in heaven, on earth or under the earth that can make that choice for you. Reading this book will not produce a pearl in you. Revelation is not transformation. Just because you now know about the different nacre responses to pain and adversity means nothing unless you actually do them. If you say you know and don't do – you don't know!

You are not alone in what you are facing. Many have gone before you and have their stories to tell. The next few chapters are stories that have been selected to encourage and inspire you to keep going; to keep reaching into God. I pray that you will see that in and through it all we can become so much more than we ever thought possible.

The pearls these stories represent are priceless, not just because of their beauty but because of the process each one has gone through to dig deep into the things of God and discover that what He says is true, who He says He is, He is, and that purpose, hope and the saving of many lives will always be on the other side of the choice to produce nacre.

The 'pearl stories' you are about to read are real. Not the fake, glossy, perfectly round pearls you can buy at a cheap market stall but genuine pearls, hallmarked by their grit and imperfect shape. These stories are powerful and valuable because they are authentic. They belong to the dark night of someone's worst storm, and are created from the choice within that storm to dive down deep; to respond with nacre and so produce a pearl of great beauty.

My prayer is that each of us would do the same; that through the pain of our personal tragedies and troubles, we would triumph in His name and produce pearls of great value. Not just to decorate our own lives with, but to bring hope and healing to many others and ultimately bring glory to the name of our redeemer, our rescuer, our Saviour, the greatest pearl pain ever produced: Jesus Christ.

From Pain to Pearls

Chapter 11: A Pearl Called Restoration

My name is Karen. It's Christmas Eve 2013, and I've just woken up next to my husband of 18 years. We have three beautiful children. I am in love with this sleeping man, warm beside me. If this was the movies, my life could look like a romantic idyllic picture, but it hasn't always been this way. What we now have has been hard fought for and hard earned, and yet as I lay here in the quietness of the morning I wonder how I can re-tell some of my story, since it feels like it must have happened to someone else. Such is the healing and restoration we have encountered by the grace of our Father God.

I wonder if I should even start digging it back up again: this pearl, so painfully wrought in the darkness, dare I open up my shell to reveal it? But then I remember standing at my kitchen sink some 12 years ago with tears pouring down my face, trying to think of someone who had experienced my pain and my challenge – and came up with a big fat no one. So for you, whoever you are, I open up my shell to show you a pearl called restoration.

Our story is one too many of us share: adultery. It is a destructive force in humanity and as ancient as time. Many of us are touched by it. The betrayal of love and all the deceit that walks with it seems to hurt a human heart like nothing else, especially when you are both Christians and serving, even leading, in church.

Mine, unlike so many of the women I have supported over the years is different, on the basis that my husband was – at least –

repentant. So, as a Christian woman married to a Christian man, I had a different journey to navigate: reconciliation. Not easy. It is one thing, forgiving and moving on to rebuild your separate lives, but it is an altogether different thing to forgive, and then to go back to an intimate, trusting relationship with the same man that betrayed you to the core.

Still, it was that journey that in **my** circumstances I felt I had to take. I had to try the long road of forgiveness ... building trust and falling in love again.

Our first daughter was three months old when my husband of seven years admitted to me one morning that he had been having an affair for a year with a woman in his office. I literally fell on the floor. The entire time we had planned our first child, the entire duration of my pregnancy and even after the birth of our princess, he had been in love and in lust with another woman.

I struggle to even find words to describe the feelings of such betrayal: crushed, broken, fighting a myriad of lies, disgust, horror, utter hatred, anger, anguish ... all of these, quickly followed by self-loathing, self-pitying and then total numbness.

With hindsight I can say that I was lucky. I didn't find him out with a seedy text or receipt. He came clean to come clean. Wracked with his own remorse, guilt, shame and pain, he was left with no other choice than to confess, make right and ask for my forgiveness.

So while he got it all off his chest to me (and then to God: I could hear the pouring out of his heart with loud wailing and tears, night after night in the spare room), I went on my own journey.

I stood in the shower crying out to God. I heard Him say to me 'If you let Me, I can fix this.

After I picked myself up from the floor, I stood in the shower crying out to God. I heard Him say to me 'If you let Me, I can fix this,' a statement I have held Him to – as He has with me – for the last 12 years.

'If you let Me': what does that mean, if **I** let you? Certainly I need **You** to fix this, but I don't even know how **to** let You; and what has any of this got to do with **me**? I am the victim here: he deserves punishment, not forgiveness. He needs to feel the consequences of his actions.

And it was that justifiably human thought that provoked the Holy Spirit to correct me. Quickly and decisively.

'I saw every sinful act. I heard every lie; and I have forgiven him. He stands made clean, holy, even pure. Who do you think you are, to stand in judgment when I have released him of his debt of sin?'

Let me tell you, that was tough to hear. Tough to comprehend and tough to process. Who was I to stand in judgement? I had to forgive. I had no right to judge, to accuse. He was forgiven, made clean. Free.

And with every day of my resentment and forgiveness and pain, I was bound. Painfully bound. It was like a poison inside that was eating me up. I couldn't even breathe for the emotion I felt. And him? He was let off, scot-free?

121

I cried (many times) to God, to help me to forgive; and He did (and still does). I finally understood the verse where Jesus says to 'forgive 77 times' (Matthew 18:22), because forgiveness is not a single act: it's a process. It is a state of being that takes you through every day.

There were two fundamentals that I believe enabled me to release the nacre of forgiveness and not only save my marriage but save myself:

Firstly, I had to understand that 'we are all sinners; we all fall short' (Romans 3:23), and to that end, I was no better than him. I had needed God's forgiveness when I became a Christian, and I knew God had accepted me, forgiven me and made me new.

So I knew we stood side by side on the 'deserve judgement' line: but instead, we had both received grace and forgiveness. That single revelation changed everything; it made me humble. It took away the need for punishment and levelled the playing field. It left me unable to wave a finger of judgement, criticism and accusation. Yes, he had done wrong against me and His Father God, but hadn't we all? 'If you don't forgive, God doesn't forgive you' (Matthew 6:15). Well, I certainly needed God's forgiveness ... so how could I even consider not forgiving for my own sake, if nothing else?

I also learnt that forgiving him didn't mean what he did was ok: what he had done wasn't ok and never would be. **But** it was not for me to hold him responsible. And forgiving him didn't mean I was letting him off lightly or being weak.

Second, I released forgiveness. I actually spoke it out. I said, 'I choose to forgive you'. It was an act of my will **not** an emotional response. It was not a romantic, smoochy moment.

It was raw but it was real. Some months later, I actually got a bucket of water, knelt down and washed his feet as a physical signal to myself, him and our enemy, the accuser, that I had chosen of my own free will to forgive and wipe him clean.

From the moment I made that decision, God released a healing balm.

It took months, if not years, for my emotions to catch up with my choices but from the moment I made that decision, God released a healing balm that soaked my very heart in peace and love. The 'divine exchange' that occurred has led me to believe that forgiveness is powerfully medicinal to human pain. But the process of actually walking out that forgiveness and learning to live together in unity was for a very long time, like a never-ending battle for my mind.

Every hour, sometimes every minute, I would be overcome with a memory or thought that would trigger a pain response in me. As if a flaming arrow had been fired, I would suddenly remember a phone call or an absence or an intimate moment we had shared that was now so poisoned that it would take me back to those first moments of pain and anguish.

There were times when I felt I was almost mentally ill. The only tonic was forgiveness, so quite literally I would have to choose to forgive **every** thought. One by one, I would nullify their power with the word of God. I had posted notes above my oven, above my sink, in the bathroom, next to my bed – all reminding me that David has been made holy, that we have all fallen short, that we had to forgive each other. They helped me to 'take captive every thought and bring it into obedience' (2 Corinthians 10:5). Replacing lies with truth was my weapon to slay every negative thought.

I didn't realise till many years later that I had learned to 'renew my mind' as the scriptures describe; this was, at times, like having a full-time job.

Day by day and month by month, the thoughts were fewer and the pain reduced. That is not to say sometimes that I wouldn't have a blow-out, but we worked hard at building trust. He communicated better and became transparent with his diary and daily commitments. He was home when he said he would be. He tried really hard to reassure me.

I navigated most of this journey without much support: my mother had died the previous year and I was far too ashamed to talk about what had happened to my friends and family. The upside of this was God became my counsellor, and He guided me skilfully through this unhappy period of my life with slow, sure steps. It's only now, as I look back, that I realise how shame stopped me getting the support I needed and only recently have I been able to unpick some emotional scars with the help of a great counsellor and through prayer ministry. My advice would be, don't go it alone.

So, my pearl? Well, it's my restored marriage and my whole family. I have a husband, he has a wife. Our children have parents who are in love. **It is as simple and as complicated as that.** A twenty-first century miracle. 12 years later, I can truly confess that God can restore marriages; if you are prepared to let him.

Chapter 12: A Pearl Called Legacy

My name is Rob. I am 31 years old, happily married and have two young children. I had a good childhood with a mum, dad and two brothers. As a family, we would just go to church at Christmas and Easter but at the age of 18, I was the first one in our household to give my life to Jesus. Since then everyone else has come to know Christ too!

At 21 years of age, I married a fabulous woman who I could build a life and a family with. We were young and as marriage tends to do, it turned the spotlight on our character flaws and issues. Using the analogy of the oyster, I suppose my irritation became myself! One of the things that can get on the inside of the oyster is a little piece of sharp shell that's broken off and becomes just as dangerous to the oyster's core as a foreign object. For me, living in such close proximity to another person revealed how out of control my emotions were.

I was angry pretty much all of the time. Mostly I would hide it and be quietly simmering away and then before I knew it, the radiator was off the wall and I had a broken foot. I did not like this 0-60MPH emotion, but I didn't quite know what to do with it or how to sort it out. And because it was happening on the inside of me; because it wasn't an external crisis but an internal one, I was able to hide it behind a fake Christian 'everything is fine' plastic smile. Whenever anyone would ask how I was doing and how life was, I would respond, 'it's fantastic'.

I have always been a firm believer that 'what you don't deal with, your kids will have to deal with'. If I didn't sort out this anger and passive aggression then my kids would have to deal with it by having a dad who they were scared of or a dad who couldn't give them the emotional intelligence they needed.

God has spoken to me many times throughout my life through the Bible, books, other people, films or just gut instinct but on two occasions He has spoken to me out loud. An audible voice that I could hear. It was around this time He spoke his first instruction to me: *'I want you to be a great husband and a great father'*. That was it. No further instruction. No to-do list or how-to manual. Just to be a great husband and a great father.

So now what? I felt that I needed to provide for my family, as probably every man does. I needed to bring home money and provisions for my household. I did have a job but they were just various temping agency jobs in the education sector and I didn't feel that there were any prospects there. Not the type of job that would support my wife and any future children we might have.

I was left everyday with a question burning in me: 'Do I have what it takes?' And I didn't know if I did.

I was left everyday with a question burning in me: 'Do I have what it takes?' And I didn't know if I did.

Strong feelings of inadequacy and even depression began to form inside of me; another internal irritation with the potential to slowly erode me from the inside out. I needed a response: something more effective than 'I'm ok, thanks'. I needed help.

My wife had suggested that I would benefit from some ministry. Some time away to pray through events and situations that had left me wounded and scarred. I didn't want to go as I didn't feel I was that messed up and in my mind, only messed up people get ministry. What would other people think? What would my friends think? But after I thrashed it out with God, it came to a point where I didn't care what others thought.

So I booked myself onto a week-long healing ministry course 200 miles from home. I did not want my future children to carry the same weight and burdens that I did, so the answer was simple: swallow your pride and start the journey to become what God had asked me to be: a great husband and great father.

I felt healed in so many areas. I no longer felt angry or trapped.

We were only in our second year of marriage and I was 23 years old and I remember the ministry very clearly. It was hard. It was upsetting at times and joyful at others. Digging up old hurts, family patterns, and past mistakes was not easy but the presence of God was so powerful and I really connected with the Holy Spirit for the first time. God helped me to identify the lies that I had been believing and showed me the truth of His word so I could start to live free again. It was a beautiful week.

On the way home in the car I remember my wife saying that I looked visibly different and that my face had changed. I felt healed in so many areas. I no longer felt angry or trapped. The radiators were now safe in my house and would not get kicked again (and my toes were safe as well!). But it was still a process.

Just like learning to walk, I had to learn new things in life: like talking to my wife and telling her how I felt. I remember having to force the words out of my mouth: 'I feel that...' It's something that I wasn't good at, but with healing came a lighter burden and it became easier every time I said it.

Soon after this, when my wife and I were 24 years old, we started to try for children. A few years went by and we had not yet been successful. We both found this incredibly hard and the overriding emotion that kept flaring up in me was bitterness, anger and betrayal. I aimed a lot of this anger at God. We were good people. Why weren't we getting pregnant? Why was the 15 year old at the school that I work at getting pregnant and then aborting the baby and we couldn't even conceive? Come on God...!!!

After just over two years of this, I was really struggling. Then the question hit again: 'Do I have what it takes?' I thought, well no, I don't. I can't even get my wife pregnant. What sort of man am I? Friendships had failed and I felt lonely, angry and totally done. Done with it all. Done with life. I just wanted to run away: pack a bag and hide in the mountains for a few months.

The tipping point of all this was one cold night in January. I felt I had been badly let down by someone close to me and emotions were hitting over and over again. Betrayal. Rejection. Bitterness. Anger. Sadness. I was sitting on my bed sobbing. Proper, pathetic sobs. Out loud I told God that I was done with all this. I was done with being put through the mill. I wanted out. I did not want His help and I was done with all this 'character building'. I would be better off not being a Christian. My wife sat and prayed with me as I had run out of things to say.

She said that God wanted to show me a picture. I closed my eyes and spoke to God through the tears to show me the picture. He showed me a very clear picture. It was a huge oak tree. It was standing on its own in a field. A storm was hitting it but the tree was hardly moving. It was so steadfast with its roots and the strength of the trunk that it was practically laughing at the storm. The oak tree was not moving, not worried and totally secure.

I asked God if the tree represented me. He said 'No'.

I asked God to show me what the picture meant. He told me that it was my son.

I asked God to show me what the picture meant. He told me that it was my son. He reminded me of my saying 'what you don't deal with, your kids will have to deal with'. He said He was teaching, training and moulding me so that my son would not have to do the same. I was making a way for my son. The oak tree was my son.

This totally broke me and as I told my wife what God had said, she just kept saying over and over 'We have a son', 'We have a son'. That night we named our son Reuben (which means 'behold we have a son') Gabriel ('man of God').

It was another year before we fell pregnant. But all the time we knew what God had said; we knew that we would fall pregnant at some point and this journey would be worth it. On 13th November 2009, our daughter was born. She was named Ariella Fae. Ariella means 'God's lioness'. Fae means 'determined faith'. God's lioness with determined faith. And at only four years old, she is definitely living up to that promise. On 23rd August 2011, our promised son was born and we named him Reuben Gabriel.

Life is good. I enjoy my job and every day I get to make a difference in the lives of young people as a Head of Year at a high school. I attend a great church and have some great friends. I love to get out and experience God in nature. In the mountains. In the wild. I get out a few times a week to fell run and I have a weekend away every six weeks to wild camp and escape the busyness of everyday life. I thank my wife for the freedom she gives me to do this. I have two wonderful children who bring a lot of joy to my life and I am sure baby number three will be on the way soon.

The Bible talks about God being the potter and us being the clay as He moulds us into what He wants us to be. It is a lovely image, and I find it quite peaceful. But sometimes God is the ironmonger. He turns the heat up, gets out the hammer and blade and starts to go to work on you, your soul, your character, your heart. It is not pretty. It is hot, sweaty, dirty, painful, but it is totally safe and done with the most love you can ever imagine. And the finished product is a beautiful creation from God. You will be healed. You will be free.

The pain of this process within me, the pain of learning to trust and to step out in faith has produced a pearl of great worth. I have fought these battles within my own soul to hand over a life of peace to my children. Like King David who fought and conquered the nations on each of his borders, in order to hand Solomon a kingdom at peace, I have been able to produce a pearl called 'legacy' – a pearl that was produced on the inside of

130

me but whose value is seen on the outside, both now and into the next generation. And for that I can only give glory to God.

From Pain to Pearls

.

Chapter 13: A Pearl Called Hope

My name Gemma means 'precious and valuable jewel' and so the concept of turning pain into pearls is a very significant one to me. There are many times in my life when I have had to choose to respond with nacre to countless intrusions of pain and trauma and yet here I am with a string of pearls as it were, able to give God all the glory for His miraculous power to transform.

Only a God who stands for love can turn darkness into light.

Only a God who stands for love can turn darkness into light, fear into faith, despair into hope and pain into something of value and worth.

Let me tell you about the pearl which for me, has been the most difficult to form, not because of God's unwillingness to heal but because of my resistance to deal with and face the depth of my hurt. I don't really know how long it takes for a grain of sand to be turned into a pearl, but I know in my own life that a pain which has taken many years to become a pearl has been my inability to conceive a child.

Growing up, there were many grains of sand in my heart that needed God's healing. Divorce and single mothers were rife in my family and the community around me. My dad left when I was five years old, leaving the way open for a violent and dangerous stepfather and resulting in an alcoholic mother and drug-addicted sister.

One of the ways I coped with these wounds was by focusing on my future and doing all I could do to get out of the environment I was in. Even though I was being bullied at school, I kept my focus. I believed education would give me a way out. I didn't want to be a teenage mother or have a child as soon as I could. I had a plan. I wanted to get an education, earn money and leave the council estate and crime-infested life I'd grown up in.

I'd sit for hours planning my dream home, imagining what my children's nursery would look like, and my children's names. I'd dream of a husband who would never leave, a man who would want children as much as I did. My dream of motherhood was to give a child everything I had lacked but so desperately desired: security, stability and safety. My desire to be a mother and give a child a different life to the one I had lived became my main motivation.

I had learned to function with dysfunction.

But when I was 15, I found out I'd never be able to conceive or carry a child. I was born without parts of my reproductive system and the parts I did have were damaged by infection and complications. The news devastated me and I became suicidal. People would say to me, 'you can adopt', but they didn't understand that to me, that was like saying to someone who has lost a limb, 'it's fine you can have a false one'.

By the time I became a Christian about 12 years ago, I was a messed up, damaged young woman on a cocktail of medication, barely living. I had learned to function with dysfunction and I had convinced myself this world was so bad that it was good I couldn't have children. I had found for a time working with babies and children a helpful way to emotionally self-harm until the pain became too evident to those around me.

For many years after finding Jesus, I refused to take this issue to Him; I didn't want to look at the beliefs and lies I had grown too comfortable with, believing this was a punishment I had to endure. I believed I didn't deserve children like most other women. I believed that no man would want a wife who couldn't give him his own children and that it would be wrong of me to deprive a man of fatherhood, even if he did.

With God's help I've learnt to respond to this particular 'grain of sand' with many coats of nacre and it all started with a promise from scripture:

> "'Sing, barren woman, you who never bore a child; burst into song, shout for joy, you who were never in labour; because more are the children of the desolate woman than of her who has a husband," says the Lord.'

Over the years God has given me more and more from Isaiah 54, but it all began with these few lines and a sense of hope, purpose and meaning beyond my own comprehension. I found comfort in this promise, even if at first I didn't understand what it meant.

After several years of being a Christian, I hit rock-bottom. My marriage fell apart and I had an extra-marital relationship that nearly destroyed myself and those around me. I had a choice:

take God at His word or die. Surrender my pain and my brokenness and trust in the Lord and His promises, or give in. I had, over the years, suffered with long periods of depression and always forced my way back through my sheer determination to not become another statistic, but God offered me a different way.

I allowed myself to become vulnerable and to admit the fear and the pain.

I allowed myself to become vulnerable and to admit the fear and the pain. Through people He placed around me, He rebuilt my heart, my life and my relationship with Him and others – including my husband, who I was apart from for five years.

God has been true to His promise and has blessed me with many 'daughters' whom I have had the privilege of loving, supporting and nurturing. I receive cards, flowers and words of gratitude every Mothers Day, thanking me for the love and care I have given out, which is nothing compared to the honour it's been to be a part of their lives.

My home has a room that's just for someone who needs love and acceptance to come and live until they are ready to wear their own pearls instead of pain. I get to offer comfort, nurture, acceptance, safety, security, stability, fun, warmth and of course a mother's love.

I feel no loss or lack. I feel I have purpose and something uniquely gifted to me from God. The pain I wore for many years has been turned by a God of hope into countless possibilities – a beautiful pearl; a gem of God's glory for the world to see.

From Pain to Pearls

Chapter 14: A Pearl Called Patience

I love the concept of finding pearls in our pain, as I believe it is the very heartbeat of God for our lives. The Bible tells us that, **'in this life we will have struggles and endure hardship'** but Jesus encourages us by saying, **'I have overcome the world!' (John 16:33)** The truth that you and I must hold onto in the midst of challenge is the fact that, seasons come and seasons go, but God is doing something beautiful in our lives to create a pearl out of our pain. Let me tell you my story.

I'd never experienced pain like it ... this was excruciating! I was writhing around on my bed, shouting in agony at the top of my voice. My wife thought I'd gone mad, she didn't know what to do with me. Between my shouts of pain and laboured breathing, I cried out to God but there was no answer.

I couldn't walk into the hospital; instead I was wheeled inside in a wheelchair.

It was so bad, my wife called a couple of friends to come over and pray for me believing for God's hand of healing and intervention. We had no idea what was wrong. I'd taken many pain-killers to ease the pain, but nothing seemed to work. It was time to go to hospital, so off we went! I couldn't walk into the hospital; instead I was wheeled inside in a wheelchair, groaning in agony. The nurse took one look at me and rushed me through for help so I was able to receive some proper pain relief.

139

After having morphine and getting an ultrasound the nurse quickly determined that I was passing kidney stones. Now ladies forgive me, and don't shout me down when I mention this, but apparently the pain of passing kidney stones is similar to that of childbirth. That's what the doctors told me ... my wife disagrees, but there you go!

Up until that point I never really thought about how I felt physically; I had experienced great health during my life, but it seemed as though this changed in my body over night.

Every few months after my first bout of kidney stones, I kept producing them and would have to have surgery to remove them. The doctors didn't know why I was producing them at such a fast rate. On more than one occasion both of my kidneys became so blocked with stones that they stopped working properly. My temperature rose dramatically and I became extremely sick due to kidney infection. I was bed-ridden for weeks. At times I was so weak that I couldn't even bring myself to walk or communicate with anyone. I would just lay in hospital, unable to move.

Extensive tests began and the doctors found that I was making a rare kind of kidney stone called a 'matrix' stone. The nature of a matrix stone is that it is not hard like other forms of kidney stones but is soft so it has a tendency to break apart in the kidney and cause a lot of tissue damage. This is why my kidneys were becoming blocked and I was passing blood. The stones are therefore a lot harder to remove and literally had to be fished out of the kidney with a tiny net.

Because I was producing this rare stone I became a focus to specialised doctors and urologists. I was told that I had a rare condition called *nephrolithiasis*. I found out that I was one of only 300 people in the UK since 1971 that had been diagnosed with this condition. Nephrolithiasis is a rare condition where the body is missing a certain gene that breaks down protein. This results in my body producing these kidney stones and the outcome is that I endure excruciating pain every few months.

This was not part of my plan. I'm sure it wouldn't be part of anyone's plan to be honest! Like most of us, I'm a busy person. I'm married with two young children and travel extensively, ministering, leading worship and speaking. So for that to be hindered by numerous operations and hospital visits on a regular basis is in no way an easy situation. I have had to develop some robust nacre responses to the invasion of this diagnosis in my life. The literal pain has somehow got to be turned into a pearl for this to be of any worth at all and so I have begun to respond from a place of faith and prayer.

Jesus always confronted sickness and disease by presenting people with a reality that was completely contrary to their condition.

As a follower of Jesus Christ and as a man who knows the Bible, I'm a firm believer that my healing, both spiritually and physically, is a done deal. The price has been paid and the work has been done for me to live in abiding health and victory. But during the early stages of this kidney condition I found that, believing something **without** resistance and believing something **with** resistance are two completely different things. Battling this rare condition in my body by standing on God's Word, became a test of faith and persistent prayer for me. They became my nacre responses.

Jesus always confronted sickness and disease by presenting people with a reality that was completely contrary to their condition. It would be up to them to have faith in Jesus' reality and decide by faith to receive it or on the other hand to accept their own condition. Jesus would never lower His standard for health and healing in a person's life just because they felt naturally unwell. He always offered a higher form of reality. I quickly learned that I too must not lower my standard of believing for breakthrough in my situation, because the reality is, **I am already healed!** I have already accepted this!

Now, it may take a while for my body to catch up with that fact but what I feel and what I experience does not change the truth and power of God's Word being able to manifest itself in my life. I have also learned that I cannot lower my expectation in God's Word to fit my experience. I must fully accept that God's Word has the power to change my experience.

I'm now 42 years of age and over the last six years there have been many opportunities for me to give up and not take God at His Word, especially in times of absolute agony. I can honestly say that there have been times where I have been upset and angry with God for allowing me to go through this journey.

As I have laid on hospital beds for weeks on end and had tubes coming out of me, draining fluid from my kidneys to protect my body from infection, I could've decided to embrace my condition and come to the conclusion that this is my lot in life. But I am determined to see things change. And let me say I'm not through it yet! I'm still believing for my body to respond to God's promise for health and healing.

Over the last six years, the pearl that has been developed in my soul is called **patience.** It's not a word we like very much at all,

142

or at least I don't. But what I've learned through my pain is that 'the testing of my faith has produced something called patience.' Or in other words the testing of what I believe to be true produces the pearl of patience to see it come to fruition. The book of James encourages us as believers to, 'let patience have its perfect work, so that we'll be perfect and complete and lacking (wanting) nothing.' (James 1:4)

God was using my condition to do a work in me.

What I failed to understand for a long time was that God was using my condition to do a work in me. Don't get me wrong, God is **not** the cause or the author of sickness, but God **can** use our painful experience and make something beautiful out of it. I have learned that patience was forging perfection and completion within me.

The fact that naturally speaking, I hadn't seen my breakthrough, caused me to stand steadfast in God and dig even deeper into Him. It caused me to be strong and tenacious and continue to declare His power and greatness in my world. Patience caused me to grow steel in my soul and it also caused me to understand Jesus and what He suffered in a whole new light.

For what value is our faith without testing? And what is hope without waiting for it with patient endurance? It's in the testing that we truly find out how strong our faith is, how likely to succeed we are and how outrageously mighty our God is.

From Pain to Pearls

My prayer for you...

In this season you may find yourself in the biggest challenge of your life. My prayer for you my friend, is that you would hold your ground and stand strong on God's Word.

I pray that you would discover your nacre responses to pain and the miracle of healing that comes from seeing that pain turned into pearls of great worth. May the pearls your life produces not only bring glory to His name but be a powerful testimony of His grace and an inspiration to all those lives your life touches.

I pray you would experience true freedom and value the journey of reaching that ultimate goal- not a life without trouble but a life that has and continues to triumph over trouble through the power of Jesus Christ.

Amen

About the Author

Arianna Walker loves adventure - which is good - as her life seems to be full of it. The best adventure is the one she's living with God, closely followed by that of being a wife, a mother, a friend, a leader, speaker, author. She believes in saying yes (evidenced by the previous list) and laughing in the face of fear (also evidenced by the list!) She loves horse riding, skiing, reading, being with her loved ones and sunshine.

Passionate about freedom, wholeness and purpose, Arianna is the Executive Director of Mercy Ministries UK and has been intricately involved in the development of Mercy Ministries in the UK since its earliest beginnings in 1999. Her younger sister, Debbie, became the first girl from the UK to graduate the Mercy programme in America years before Mercy Ministries UK existed. Seeing Debbie's life utterly transformed became a catalyst for Arianna's continued fervour and passion to see the work of Mercy Ministries established in the UK. Now, 10 years since her sister's graduation, Arianna leads the MMUK team, which includes her sister Debbie as Programme Director. Since the UK home opened its doors in 2006, more than 160 girls have had an opportunity to experience God's unconditional love, forgiveness and life transforming power.

The home based in West Yorkshire represents the beginning of Mercy Ministries' journey in the UK. With an extension completed in 2011 to increase the intake from 10 beds to 20 and more homes planned across the country, Arianna and her team remain focused on continuing to make a difference to broken lives in the UK and Europe in partnership with local churches across the nation.

From Pain to Pearls

If you would like to know more about the work of Mercy Ministries UK, if would like to apply to the programme or if you would like to invite Arianna to speak at your conference, event or church, please contact Mercy Ministries UK at: info@mercyministries.co.uk or check out the website: www.mercyministries.co.uk

You can follow Arianna on Twitter, Facebook and Instagram @AriannaWalker